LEADERSHIP IS LOVE

A PRACTICAL GUIDE FOR A RADICAL IDEA

Christopher Leonard, PsyD

Licensed Psychologist

Flint Hills Publishing

Praise for *Leadership is Love...*

"*Leadership is Love* is an honest, courageous call to lead differently. Dr. Christopher Leonard reminds us that when leaders center humanity, trust, and care, organizations become stronger—and people do too."
 –Wichita State President Rick Muma, Ph.D., MPH, PA-C

"This book reminds us that leadership has always been about people first. Through real experiences and clear, actionable lessons, *Leadership is Love* shows how leaders can replace fear and control with trust, accountability, and genuine care, and build stronger organizations because of it."

–Curt Coffman, *New York Times* best-selling author of *First, Break all the Rules: What the World's Greatest Managers Differently*

"Organizations invest heavily in preparing leaders to use structural tools—job descriptions, performance metrics, policies, corrective actions—to guide and influence human behavior. Dr. Leonard's practical and highly readable book demonstrates that relationship tools—caring, appreciation, empathy, trust, listening, and genuine understanding—are even more impactful for accelerating growth, strengthening team cohesion, and elevating performance."

-Gerald H. Graham, Ph.D., R.P. Clinton Distinguished Professor of Management at Wichita State University and author of *Lead: How Effective Leaders Get Things Done* and *High-Performance Leadership Practices*

"In this deeply authentic and experience-driven book, Dr. Christopher Leonard challenges the traditional model of leadership while offering leaders a method that encompasses selflessness, openness, and wisdom to see the humanity within the systems their team navigates daily. Drawing from real-world leadership challenges, lived experience, and psychological insight, this book calls for intentional introspection as well as purposeful responding and empowerment. With clarity, humor, and honest self-reflection, he equips leaders with practical tools to build and sustain relationships, set expectations that are meaningful and accurate, and react with empathy. *Leadership is Love* is for leaders who are ready to challenge their conventional strategies in order to lead the whole being of their workplace."

–Selena R. Jackson, Ph.D., licensed psychologist, author, & speaker

---

"This is a dope concept I'm already pulling from, and I'm excited for this blueprint to get into leaders' hands so they can step into a radical yet deeply practical way of leading. *Leadership is Love* offers tangible strategies for shaping healthier work environments and culture. Leaning into its ideas can spark truly transformational workplaces, and you can live them out daily in all your relationships."

–Danielle Johnson, MPA, Executive Director, Wichita Habitat for Humanity

Leadership is Love – A Practical Guide for a Radical Idea
©2026 Christopher Leonard, PsyD

Cover design by Amy Albright
stonypointgraphics.weebly.com

Illustrations by Samantha Tedder
Illustrations digitized by Layna Adams
Sticker designed by Victoria Hall

Flint Hills Publishing

Topeka, Kansas
Tucson, Arizona
www.flinthillspublishing.com

Paperback ISBN: 978-1-966323-58-7
Electronic Book ISBN: 978-1-966323-59-4

Library of Congress Control Number: 2026902832

Printed in the U.S.A.

To Missy,

for always believing in me more than I ever did.

CONTENTS

INTRODUCTION

The foundation of this book comes from lived experiences that are both good and bad. Many of these perspectives are from personal and witnessed experiences. From these mistakes and successes I have made or witnessed, you will be able to glean insights into how to apply these ideas at your workplace. You will also learn about some of the folks who embody these ideas. The beginning of the book is also about radical ideas. You might doubt that these ideas could ever really happen in a workplace, but trust me, it has happened. I have seen these radical ideas in action by others or myself.

I hope if you choose to implement what I share, you will experience the same or greater impact from these ideas that I have over the years. Nonetheless, you would be mistaken if you thought the significant impact I was referring to was only business success, increased profits, or productivity. The most important things you will experience if you implement these ideas are the growth of your staff and the joy they will bring to your workplace and each other's lives.

Authoring this book is about sharing what I have taken from these experiences. Additionally, you should know I am not a professional writer. So, when I decided to write this, I did not want to write a book that is research heavy. I completed graduate school and wrote enough research and scholarly papers. I find that the books I read that are too research heavy get boring or dense. I did not want you to have that experience reading this book. I just want you to know what is coming from my life and my heart. I have also read leadership books that tell these long stories with these giant arcs. Those books include some fun and flowery language. I feel those books miss the opportunity to be direct. Hence, the reason for the set-up of this book. It focuses on the practical and radical with the intention of being concise, direct, and heartfelt.

Practical

Keeping a book practical is the only way to author a book on leadership. With the busy nature of work and the demands of life, keeping this book a quick read is the only reasonable way to respect your life's needs. Easy, clear, and concise writing makes implementing radical ideas much easier. So let us talk about why radical ideas matter in leadership.

Radical

Too many business meetings, staff meetings, and organizations get stuffy. Organizations get caught up on the horizon and lose sight of the folks below on the oars. This book focuses on the folks holding the oars. This book is about helping leaders, like you, see those on the oars too. Ideally, the unorthodox nature of this book should not be viewed as radical in our organizations. But, in too many conversations in our workplaces, leaders only focus on the bottom line or only on the customer, which they see as the main goal. The main goal should be your people and the relationships you foster as a leader. This does not mean forgetting the bottom line or customers, but by focusing first on your people you will reach that horizon faster than you will ever know.

How do I know this? By living it!

PART I

The Why

An optimist, a realist, and idealist

walk into a bar...

after a couple beers, this book

would be created.

Cheers!

WHY WOULD YOU LISTEN TO ME?

I attended a professional training a couple of years ago that was about understanding change in the workplace. The speaker discussed how there is a model leaders can adopt that addresses the changes that occur at all levels within an organization. It was a great, engaging, and interesting presentation. The speaker gave a unique perspective on leadership in the workplace. At the end of the training, I asked one question:

Where is this model being applied in workplaces that I can see as a real-world example?

I wanted to know if there were organizations I could look at as a blueprint for my office. I wanted to learn how leaders were implementing what was discussed in the training. I wanted to know what worked and did not work for their workplaces. Sadly, the presenter responded that the leadership style they developed had not been applied in other workplaces or organizations.

I felt deflated.

At that moment, I came to a conclusion about how I would lead. I would never write or promote anything I have not lived, done, or led. I wrote this book to share what I have learned by experience as a leader at work. This is not a book of interviews. I did not write this book to expound theory or to conduct a literature review. This material comes from a psychologist's lived experience as a leader—reflection that explores the good and bad, joy and pain, as well as growth and aspirations that all leaders will go through.

Too often it feels like authors I read or speakers I hear, talk about ways to lead, but not how they have lived their work. So, why would you listen to me? I could tell all these reasons to listen to me and try to explain why I am an expert. But really, I do not think many of those things matter. All that I honestly think matters is that what you will read in this book are true stories and everything I suggest or encourage I lived, for better or worse in my life.

So, if you choose to continue, please take what you can. It could come in handy someday, because it has for me. Read with an open heart and reflective mind. I have found these experiences have made me a better leader, and I am grateful for that professional growth. The best thing, however, is it has truly made me a better co-worker, peer, friend, spouse, and father.

Enjoy!

WHY 'LEADERSHIP IS LOVE?"

When the leadership of others is not from love,

they lead from fear and control.

This is the biggest issue facing organizations today: leadership by fear and control. It is time to challenge the status quo and recognize that individuals are not leading well when they lead by fear and control. True leadership is love, and love has always been best. Anything else is not leadership, only cold transactions and means of domination.

The concept of leadership is love is the antithesis to fear and control. This leadership style does not view employees as cogs. It sees them with their full humanity on display. Leadership is loving them as a whole person. Now, this idea is not platonic, brotherly, romantic, familial, or self-love. Leadership is love is a version of agape love. It is centered on selflessness, wanting the best for others, empathy, and commitment to the individual's humanity.

Many individuals find the concept of love hard to define. Paradoxically, with a quick internet search, one will also see there are so many ways love is defined. I do not feel the need to make up a special definition for this book, but rather highlight the type of love that captures the spirit of leadership is love. This is my reason for using agape love to describe the heart of this leadership style.

Agape love puts the needs and welfare of others first. Agape love is seeing the wholeness of the person in front of you and engaging in compassion, respect, and care. It is not a type of love that is expected to be reciprocal, but rather a love that spreads from others who have ever received such a powerful type of love.

This is why agape love is the heart of true leadership and why leadership is love.

Leaders who apply this love in the workplace recognize that the results of this leadership don't just reward the giver. Leaders see the reward from agape love spreading throughout the office, bettering anyone who is touched by agape love's compassion, respect, and care. Thus creating a workplace where leadership is love.

Leadership that does not love creates a workplace with low staff morale and negative competition for resources. A leadership-verses-staff mentality ensues. If this describes your current workplace, leadership is love will help. It will help your organization express true leadership.

Be aware: new leaders and jaded leaders are the biggest culprits of using fear and control in the workplace. They either fear screwing up and being viewed poorly, or they have been burned too many times by disloyal or disrespectful employees and treat all staff as incompetent. Worst of all is when leaders embody both of these characteristics in their leadership. Today is the time to change this way of leadership, not just for the betterment of the organization, but for your staff.

Leadership is love does not mean all the flowery language and kumbaya that might come to your mind when thinking about love in the workplace. Rather, this is a deeper caring for the individuals we work with who are flawed but are still worthy of respect from their leadership. Leadership is love enriches our relationships in the workplace.

This leadership is selfless and is not afraid of giving hard feedback because of a desire to be liked. It is wanting the best for others and knowing the best might not be them staying in your office. It is showing up every day with empathy and a commitment to your employee's humanity, however challenging it may be for the leader.

Leadership is love becomes the truest relationship you will have with others in the workplace. In this relationship the leader fully commits to their staff, sees their humanity inside and outside of the office, and expects more from them than they ever imagined. It is not a relationship set on the pretense of control, mistrust, and fear. It is not the type of relationship commonly thought of in the workplace. Leadership is love is something different. It is bigger than the workplace—it is what connects us to each other and our humanity. It welcomes vulnerability and removes our fear and desire for control over others. Leadership is love then becomes the solution to the fear and control employees face in the workplace. If you are inclined to fear or control in your management of others, I implore you to discover how leadership is love.

PART II

The Radical Idea

Leadership is love when we…

- Think with curiosity

-Act with gratitude

- Embrace our humanity

- Dream bigger for others

LEADERSHIP IS LOVE

Leadership is love is a big idea. An idea that is multi-faceted and can seem overwhelming, unrealistic, or unhelpful to both new and seasoned leaders. Again, this is a radical idea and learning that leadership is love may seem like too much for a leader to do. Seeing leadership as love might even feel to some as burdensome.

That is exactly why realizing that leadership is love is profound and essential—radical.

If it were easy, it would be the norm right now in organizations. Since embracing leadership as love is not part of the norm right now, it is likely thought to be unrealistic to way too many leaders. However, innovative ideas are needed at radical times. I find it hard to believe right now that the workforce, YOUR workforce, is just happy as can be and has all their needs met at home AND at work. This is why we should lead with love now. This is why we need to be radical.

I know this may feel overwhelming, but I encourage you to sit with the discomfort. I also challenge the idea that you as the reader have not led with love in some other aspect of your life, or even in the workplace. You might not identify your leadership or interactions in the workplace or life as such, but you likely have led with love in one way or another. You may think this idea is unrealistic. One's ability to love always exists. Here is the question for the leaders:

Are you willing to step into the office with love?

Some might respond by saying, "That is not how the office works." Others may say, "When you do bring love into the workplace, you get burned down the road." Does that last statement sound familiar to how others talk about the different relationships they have in their lives? These statements maintain the status quo. Failing to realize that leadership is love and avoiding any risk only results in lost possibilities at work.

Loving always comes with risks.

More importantly, your workforce misses out on maximizing their potential in the office and in life.

Therefore, when you hear professionals talking about how love at work is unhelpful or not part of the work, challenge that. Why? When we exclude love from a place, what do we see? Think about it.

I will pause…

So, what comes to mind? A workplace that is warm or welcoming, or a workplace that treats the staff as cogs in a machine and is hostile to the organization? That company is somewhere I would not want to work, or recommend someone join.

Additionally, when have you ever been in a workplace or organization where leadership as love was given, and you did not enjoy that gift? The only type of organization I can think of are the ones where individuals say they do, but do not really engage in the work of love in leadership.

What does it take to recognize that leadership is love, and what does that truly look like? Well, it takes a lot of strength and courage from a leader to engage in the workplace with love. This radical way of leading comes from the key concepts which you will learn about in Part II. You will realize the importance of thinking with curiosity, acting with gratitude, embracing our humanity, and dreaming bigger for your staff. These fundamental ideas are what truly define how leadership is love. Finally, you will see the significance of workplace relationships and how they are the threads that hold all organizations together. So, let us begin.

What Is Love in Work?

This question might come with many answers but let us make this tangible. Love is the words in these chapters and how those words are applied to your organization. It is the radical ideas you will read, but also the simple solutions and behaviors in action. Simply…

Love in work is relationships.

Right! It is because this book is about relationships. All organizations that involve two or more people working together are about relationships. If you think not, you are lying to yourself. All decent work is completed by working together. Excellent work is done when love is a motivator in those relationships.

Now, these relationships are not the type of relationships you see in movies or, unfortunately, ones you read in the headlines. Nor should love in leadership ever be used to take advantage of or manipulate people. Control is the motivator in manipulation and is the opposite of leadership as love.

Love in work is about true relationships in the workplace.

True relationships are flawed, but beautiful. Just like the ones we have outside of work, relationships matter, and they can be messy. Still, remarkable things can happen through strong relationships. You see it all the time in the world and within your small groups of friends. Create love in work and see how far those relationships take you, your staff, and your organization.

Does Love Matter?

Yes, it does. Love matters a lot! If our leadership is not love, how do we lead others? I believe we lead others with indifference, control, or fear when we avoid love. Some leaders might state their leadership is just transactional and love does not matter, even if that is true for others. My question is: How do you lead when the relationship is transactional, indifferent, and devoid of caring and empathy? If you turn your staff into cogs, just part of the machinery of your business, you will deny your staff their humanity. What are you avoiding? Are you indifferent to their humanity or are you afraid of their humanity?

When leaders stay indifferent, their staff will experience that indifference throughout the organization. When leaders relate from a place of fear, staff will sense the precaution in the air. When we lead with fear, we punish our staff with a lack of trust.

Additionally, leadership is love is not an excuse to misuse the language of love as a way to control or micromanage staff. This is far from true leadership; rather it is deception and manipulation. This misuse and deception only results in turnovers, low morale, and trepidation.

One thing I reflect back on as a leader is when staff screw up. Too often I see and hear about situations where a staff member does something wrong and then the leader changes policy for everyone. That is leading from fear, not love. Addressing the mistake and helping the individual who made the mistake is leading with love, not punishing all staff. Better experiences in your organization will happen when you as a leader can step away from fear and lean into love.

Why Love Matters

Basically, the world, our workplaces, our communities, and the people in our lives need love right now. In this time, there is not a better reason to bring more love into the world. If you or I can do this at any scale, we can make a difference; I mean any scale—a workplace of three or an organization of thousands—leadership that is love can move organizations.

When leaders bring love to their organization, love spreads.

I honestly believe the world can get better one person at a time. I believe this so wholeheartedly. The world can get better one interaction at a time. This is why leading with love matters. The world and you will be better because of it.

How Do You Want to Lead?
How Do You Want to Be Led?

When I meet with new leaders, I ask these questions early on. I am always extremely interested in hearing the answers, especially to the second question. I do this because I want to listen for two things. One, how are they expecting me to manage them? Two, is the way they want to lead congruent with how they want to be led?

The second insight is important because if the way you want to be led is not the way you want to lead, then we have a problem. Rather, you have a big—and I mean big—problem. Leadership as love is not about creating different rules for you. It is about leading others the way you want to be led. So, remember…

How do you want to be led?

Be Selfless

Fundamentally, I believe selfless people focus beyond themselves and concentrate on the needs of others. Selflessness in leadership requires these behaviors and beliefs, and can still look different depending on the organization, environment, and needs of the staff in those workplaces.

So, how can leaders be selfless? Leaders need to focus on their staff's needs. Therefore, leaders must communicate with staff about their desires and needs. This requires leaders to be curious about staff instead of thinking they know what they need or want. Leaders are humble and do not pretend they know everything that a staff member wants, even if the leader was in a similar position in the past.

Selfishness is a strong temptation. It is like the last doughnut in the breakroom. The only thing that comes from it is limited joy and extra work. I gain five pounds when I smell a doughnut. Leadership is love when leaders keep their team in mind and continually think about ways that benefit the staff. I am not saying that as leaders we cannot think about ourselves. A metaphor I really lean into is the oxygen mask on the airplane. Leaders need to be reflective when putting on their oxygen mask first. And remember to get oxygen to the staff! Still, selfishness can occur easily when power is involved.

On the flipside of being selfish, as leaders we need to know the limits and maintain our boundaries. Leaders should not use the goal of not being selfish as an excuse to be a workaholic or to be a martyr in the workplace. That type of behavior only results in burnout, pain, and misery. Additionally, your staff will take cues from your behavior. Do not let your lack of boundaries spread the burnout, pain, and misery to everyone else. Your staff will not be around much longer if that continues. The worst thing a leader can do to themselves is become their own architect of an apathetic and jaded view of their own work.

As you read further you will learn that inviting others into your world and work will have a greater impact on your office. Hoarding knowledge, resources, and security are just other examples of selfishness that have no place in your organization when you are the leader. Self-interest does not move the needle with your staff, it just turns them off at work or worse. It turns your staff into self-serving employees. When you model selflessness, your staff will follow.

Model what you want to see in others.

Helpful Feedback Is Selfless and Tactful

There is a common misconception that feedback is only good when it is nice and positive. I often hear that giving feedback is hard because it might hurt the other person's feelings. I challenge that notion a lot. To me, leadership is not love when we withhold information that could help staff become better employees or better people. Now, that does not mean leaders should forget tact. Tact continues to be vital to healthy relationships in organizations.

Tact is fundamental in giving feedback.

Leadership is love when we are selfless, helping others grow, and giving feedback even when it makes us uncomfortable. Leaders who own their feedback understand leadership as love. It is knowing that right now, it might be hard to hear for the person, even with tact. Nonetheless, in the long run it will help the organization, and most importantly, help the person who you are providing feedback to. This is because leaders must do hard things, and providing helpful feedback can be a challenge. We need to learn to be comfortable with challenges. We need to remember that if we avoid challenges, we are likely being selfish.

Give It Away

I have thought plenty about leadership as love. To start this process, you first must be willing to give love to others. Leading with love is not just a thought. It is not just a feeling. It is an action. It is a selfless, empathetic act that requires attention and a willingness to continue giving it to others.

Sadly, we will give it away only when it feels safe. We will give it away when we think we will not be hurt or when it feels easy for us. Leaders need to give love away when they are scared, when a situation takes vulnerability, and when it is incredibly hard. We need to give it away in the face of hate, distrust, or apathy. Leaders are selfless when they give love, even when the environment is not encouraging such acts. Remember, bringing less love to the workplace never results in increased love for all the staff.

Leaders will also have to listen to their staff members and learn how they want to receive love as well. The goal of giving it away is no good when the person is not receiving it. This is where this book can help. Through the ideas presented, leaders will create environments that help staff become more willing to accept this type of leadership. So, learn about your staff and then you will be best equipped to lead with love.

Tell Stories and Listen to Stories

When we tell stories, we talk about history, provide context, and, if we are lucky, provide knowledge or wisdom. When we listen to stories, we gain insight into others. Our staff can learn from those stories, and we can learn about ourselves. As leaders, we are storytellers. Leaders can talk a lot, but we can learn a lot more from being quiet. As you build relationships with staff members, you will be surprised to see how much the quality of our workplace relationships impact storytelling. Through the strength of the relationships those stories get more detailed, deeper, and personal.

The beauty of the stories we hear and tell in the office is how those stories can be our benchmark for comfort. Think about it for second. What stories or topics do you discuss only with family? What stories do you discuss only with friends? What stories did you finally start opening up about at work? I bet you can think of a couple you have or a couple you almost shared. That is a great barometer of your feelings of connectedness in the workplace. Be mindful of the stories you are telling and make sure to listen to your staff.

An easy test for you to gauge your comfort in your workplace is this following thought experiment. Think of a recent story you told for the first time in your workplace. Would you have told that on your first day? Would you have told that story at your last job? Finally, if you have not told a story recently in your workplace, think about what that means.

Mentor and Be Mentored

When we mentor, we grow our staff, but we also grow ourselves. We learn deeper about our staff's wants and desires. This is a precious relationship that can grow into a lifelong relationship, partnership, and most importantly, be passed down to the next person looking to be mentored.

Generational wisdom occurs, which is one of the best ways to create a stable culture.

One of the greatest things I provide as a licensed psychologist is one hour of weekly clinical supervision. I used to think it was a lot of work, but now I see it as a gift. The reason is easy. Clinical supervision allowed me to really get to know my staff, and more than that, I continued to learn about myself as a leader. The ability to mentor and see the growth right in front of my eyes is one of the most rewarding things a leader can experience. Some of the greatest things within my supervision time with staff are the stories we tell each other. The beauty of mentoring is you do not need clinical supervision to be a mentor. Being a mentor can happen over lunch, in the hallway, or on a walk. Leadership as love occurs when you give your time to make others better.

History, knowledge, and experience are often passed down verbally. The staff meetings in my office make this happen. How does your organization pass along information? How often do you read a policy and procedures manual and truly understand how an organization runs?

I didn't think so.

However, you will quickly learn from a mentor about company culture, the ins and outs, and—most importantly—who makes the best baked goods! That is why being mentored is just as important as being a mentor.

Being mentored allows you to learn your blind spots within the organization. The mentor can see your organizational leadership weaknesses and coach you through them. They can pick up on your personal challenges and see you as a human. They can be your sounding board. When you have mentors outside of your organization who have led before, they can help you with your general leadership skills and bring to the relationship a fresh perspective. Leadership is love works because leaders are still willing to learn, and a mentor worth their weight will help you continue to learn about leadership, yourself, and life. I highly recommend leaders find their mentor and learn. Remember, leading takes the willingness to try something different, to push ourselves and others, and seeing the best in others. Be that for someone and find your mentor.

Thus, leaders succeed when they bring the humanity of their staff into the workplace. Leaders who focus on the relationship between leadership and employees unleash the true potential of their staff. This is because leadership as love not only changes the people and relationships within the workplace, but improves workplace culture, organizational output, and the world.

THINK WITH CURIOSITY

Curiosity starts with a nonjudgmental mindset. A non-judgmental mindset, in my eyes, is when individuals do not default to interpretations of behaviors or experience an emotion as fact. Instead, individuals holding a nonjudgmental mindset stay curious about situations, including actions of others and their own actions. They remain open to multiple perspectives of events rather than the first reaction.

When we judge, we add our own views to the situation that are not based on objective observations. Leaders' judgments of actions or events in the workplace can be influenced by their past experiences, values/beliefs, current sensations and thoughts, or a combination of any of these influences. Hence, highlighting the importance of leaders being aware of how their past experiences, values/beliefs, and sensations and thoughts in the current moment impact their ability to take a nonjudgemental stance within the workplace.

Curiosity Creates an Open Mind

As a leader, it becomes easy over time to make educated guesses based on prior experiences. When I find myself in these situations, I do not disregard these thoughts. I just treat those intuitions as hypotheses and still approach the situation with curiosity. Leadership as love happens when leaders stay curious about situations rather than default to an assumption. When approaching staff with foredrawn conclusions, our tone, interactions, and situational outcomes are almost decided before the conversation even begins. Coming to these interactions with an open mind and a curiosity to understand the other person's perspective is when leadership is love.

Again, as you will see through this book, things need to be qualified. Perhaps after reading that last paragraph you will be asking all these questions in your head and thinking this is naïve or unrealistic. Two challenges to this thought come to my mind. One, the reason this feels unrealistic is because it goes against the status quo. Two, when leaders engage in leadership as love, they are never being naïve, they are actually rather strategic. What makes this different from other ways of leadership is that some of the strategy is giving up control and not having the answers beforehand. Thinking with curiosity highlights the latter point. So, here are some ways you as a leader can think with curiosity in your organization.

Don't Assume or Jump to Conclusions

Your goal is to not come to meetings with foredrawn conclusions. Assumptions just lead to a vacuum of knowledge in your organization. Hoarding knowledge in the workplace is likely a death sentence to an organization when the industry shifts. The result is the loss of innovation for everyone in the workplace and in your development as a leader. Without curiosity, you can misplace office priorities and miss investments in new assets for your workplace or in staff.

For example, leaders can pass over a staff member for promotion because we might think they have no interest in the expanded role. Instead of just concluding that that individual would not want or not be good in the position, explore the possibility as a mental experiment or explore their interest by talking with the employee.

Sadly, jumping to conclusions results in one of the worst things that can happen with your staff, and that is the loss of empathy. There are important moments in the workplace when empathy is needed with your staff. When you think with curiosity and do not jump to conclusions, empathy has a chance to help you lead with love.

Hold Judgement and Don't Assume Ill Intent

Judgement and assuming ill intent are office morale killers—period. When leaders engage in this behavior with a staff member, that particular staff member checks out. When your staff sees that this occurred to one or more staff members, they check out too. The message you send is that your staff cannot be trusted. They then will believe that you, as their leader, cannot be trusted. This becomes a death spiral for you. Also, you are the only one who can get out of it. There is no motive or gain for your staff to change their view of you. They show up and just continue to collect their paycheck or leave to go where trust is valued. So, as leaders you must establish a good faith approach in your workplace.

Good Faith Approach

Organizations that create a good faith approach establish a culture where behaviors, statements, and omissions are not seen as coming from a place of harm. This does not mean feelings cannot hurt. It means the intentions of the person were not to hurt individuals in the office. Changes within the organization with funding, structure, or attention were not targeted toward individuals or units for petty or interpersonal reasons. The reality of the good faith approach is that leaders and employees know they will mess up. It is the nature of being human. However, with a good faith approach in the office, grace is given to the individual who messes up. I do not know any leader who would not want to be afforded some grace when they mess up. Knowing that...

Are you giving grace to others when they make mistakes?

One story of good faith in action for me is when I messed up and mispronounced a staff member's name at a whole-division event. It was one of those breakfasts where each department has their leader stand up and introduce all the new members since the last breakfast. These happen about once every six months or so. It's a fun time, and they always provide extra bacon for the group!

So, it's my turn to stand up and state all the names. I really hate this part because I never want to forget a name. Sometimes we hire people right after the last breakfast and they integrate into our team so well I forget they have been in our department for less than six months. So, I'm prepping for the breakfast, double checking with my staff to make sure I have figured out everyone I need to introduce. I do this every breakfast, and at this specific breakfast, I mispronounce the name by adding an emphasis on one part of the name when it was not needed. This was the mistake I didn't even realize I'd made.

After the breakfast, the staff member pulled me aside and let me know of the mistake. The funny part was that the staff member had to work hard to teach me how to pronounce their last name. Sadly, it took about three to four times for me to even hear the difference. Nevertheless, that is me. I have been terrible with names my whole life. Still, that is never an excuse to not fix it in the future.

What happened next is why real leadership is love and love works. I apologized because I was in the wrong. The staff member, taking a good faith approach, understood my error, did not hold that error against me, and saw that I cared to make it right. My favorite part of this story is looking back and thinking about all the ways this interaction could have gone wrong, and yet it did not. As a leader, I could have felt attacked and dismissed the concern of the staff member. The staff member on the other hand could have felt that I was diminishing their importance in the workplace, and worse, targeting them. The worst outcome would have been the staff member not even bringing it up to me because of a lack of trust in the relationship. I am grateful for the grace the staff member gave me in that moment. I am grateful that I was able to have this moment with my staff member to make it right.

An example of a lack of good faith in the office is one I experienced many years ago. There was a coworker who spoke a lot about sports in the office; we'll call her Jill. So, a professional team was about to be swept in a playoff series that year. The next day after the team went down 0-3 in the series, I entered our staff meeting at the office. I saw Jill sitting at the conference table. I walked in and stated, "Time to get the broom." A couple other coworkers saw this, and to my and her surprise, they asked, "Did you just tell her to get a broom?" in a scolding tone. Jill and I, then in a panic of confusion, had to explain ourselves to everyone in the room to defuse the implications of sexism in the workplace. That was a moment when good faith assumptions did not exist. There was no curiosity about the interaction, or evidence of the interpersonal connection Jill and I had. In a workplace where there is good faith and curiosity, this scenario can exist, but the interaction would be completely different.

Learn from Others

One of the best things that can happen from thinking with curiosity is learning from one another. When done right, you get their perspective. This can give you insight into others and help you grow. When learning from others spreads in the workplace, your whole organization grows. Learning from others within your organization is a wonderful way to grow within your workplace culture, but do not limit yourself to just learning from others in your organization.

Be a sponge.

When I have an opportunity to gain experience and knowledge from others outside of my field, I lean in. I love to learn the ins and outs of team sports, politics, business, history, philosophy, space, and the arts. I was inspired to write this book after reading so many books on leadership. Anytime new information is provided on ways of doing things, or about things that I have no knowledge of, I am curious about how this may apply to my life or work. When you are open to others and are willing to read, listen, or observe, your world will be enriched. I encourage you to be enriched, but that takes a leader who is open to learning from others.

Consult with Others about Your Thoughts

Thinking with curiosity is not a default for many individuals. I would say it is not a default for me. So, when situations happen where I have initial thoughts, I always pause and remind myself to think with curiosity. As a leader, I also consult with colleagues about my initial thoughts and remind myself to be curious. Most importantly, I listen to staff when they have an initial thought about a situation. I then instruct them to still approach the situation with curiosity. What I have found is that checking in with someone (likely a peer) creates opportunities to reset and remind ourselves leadership is love, and approach the next situation with curiosity.

THINK WITH CURIOSITY

Profiles of Inspiration

Lana Anthis

Born 1968

Lana is a Wichita State University human resources business partner. She has worked at Wichita State University for more than ten years. Her love for the past and her desire to see a better future are some of the reasons I feel so connected to her. Lana is my go-to person in Human Resources for my job. She is an absolutely wonderful and interesting person. So, it is funny for me when I tell people I like talking with Human Resources. With all the great aspects of Lana, the thing I admire about her most is her ability to withhold judgment and remain curious. Because of that ability, she was the inspiration for this chapter.

So, how did this all happen? It all started when I went to her about challenges I was facing in the workplace as a new leader. In my first leadership position, I was hesitant to reach out to Human Resources, but after talking with Lana a couple times, it became clear; she was there to help. She helped most by stressing the need to withhold judgment and explore the issue first, and to not go into conversations with predetermined views or assumptions. In those moments, I grew so much and became a better leader because of her influence. She had such an impact on me when I was early into my leadership roles.

Nicholas Leonard

Born 1982

Nicholas, "Nick," Leonard is an interesting one. The reader might notice the same last name. Well, he is my brother. So, this inspiration of memories and influence is one I have had in my life for more than thirty years. His impact on my life is the fact that he has always looked at multiple ways to understand situations. He has never approached anything with a closed mind. It is something I have admired about him for a long time. Nick is impressive because he has opened my mind to so many different perspectives with his willingness to allow different perspectives in his worldview at the same time.

Nick is always open to the possibilities of life, whether it was moving to New York City or Los Angeles. He has taken risks his whole life to find opportunities. In our multi-hour phone calls as adults, and late nights as kids, we discussed life, its meaning, and how the world works. That is where I would witness his beliefs in action. I cherished those memories of a future for the better in those conversations. Because in those moments, he and I would just want to learn more about the why and how of the world. How we approached those conversations still impacts my life today. They remind me that people are always more complex than a simple answer and learning a person's reason is more powerful than assigning a reason.

ACT WITH GRATITUDE

Thank you!

Thank you for giving your time to this read. I hope this is a meaningful experience and, in some way, meets your expectations. I am grateful for time you are giving me.

The world has seemed to harden in the past ten years. It also seems that this shift toward a hardened world has now become an excuse for leaders to act that way as well. Therefore, when leaders act with less humility and gratitude, the world and the workplace become more transactional, distant, and cold. So, when you are out in front as the leader, the best you can do is to lead with gratitude as an example for others. Acting with gratitude is another hallmark of leadership as love. One of the best things about acting with gratitude is it not only helps others feel appreciated, but it also helps you feel more connected to the world. Make someone seen for their good work and contribution to the organization. The impact of being seen can go on in their life beyond that interaction and is truly never measurable.

So, let's dive into two major ways to act with gratitude. But before we do that, let us take a moment to recognize the importance of time.

The Gift of Time

When someone gives you their time, they are giving you a gift. Time might even be the most priceless gift. I believe this for the simple reason that though time is universal and everyone has it, the amount is limited. You can never get it back and you do not know how much time you will have in your life.

So, when someone gives time to you, they are giving you part of their life that they will never get back.

If you think there is a price tag on a person's time, I am surprised you are even reading this book. For those who do agree with me about time, are you allowing yourself to lean into the gift? Leading with love recognizes the gift of time in your workplace and relationships with family and friends. Leaders are grateful for others who give their time and knowledge to them.

Say Thank You

It is quite easy to say those two words. It also never hurt you when you thanked someone. I will even give you a minute to reflect.

How was it? Right!

Saying thank you does not hurt you as a leader. So, say it frequently and say it with inflection. The impact you can have on someone and their day by noticing their work for you or others is a seismic culture changer. That is the beauty of caring—it can be contagious. Be Patient Zero in your organization and watch caring spread.

For the leaders who think saying thank you does not make a difference, I challenge this with some concessions. Again, I am not completely naïve. So here are my concessions.

A thank you does not replace the following:

- Bonuses

- Compensation

- Time off

Also, that does not mean you should stop saying thank you. It means that leaders need to recognize what a thank you means at its core. A thank you is an emotional expression of gratitude. The use of thank you statements is not meant to be a replacement of those concessions above. Leaders who use a verbal thank you in place of the above concessions need to work on those issues they are masking. Leaders who continue to misuse a thank you weaken the message's impact in the moment. When leaders do that, they engage in misuse of the power of a thank you, further weakening their message over time. Even the impact of a meaningful thank you deteriorates for the individuals receiving the message.

Don't be that leader.

Appreciate Folks No Matter Their Title

So much joy can enter a person's life when you appreciate them. No matter how big or small the action, statement, or gesture someone makes toward you, people flourish from appreciation. Therefore, I truly detest when folks think that different positions deserve various levels of respect. As leaders, everyone in your organization matters, and everyone, no matter how they contribute to your organization, deserves appreciation.

When leadership is love, leaders now can see how to act with gratitude. This idea and these behaviors all add to creating a culture where your staff's efforts are seen and appreciated. As a leader, acting with gratitude is one of the easiest ideas to engage with. It is also one of the most rewarding ideas in this book. The best part is it is rewarding to receive gratitude as well as give it.

Like I said earlier, in the first chapter, give it away. If you do, it only gets better for everyone.

ACT WITH GRATITUDE

Profiles of Inspiration

Janet Malooley

Born 1923

Janet Malooley was a licensed registered nurse, but more importantly, she was my godmother and great aunt. She was of a petite stature, but her kindness was giant. Throughout her life, I never saw a moment where she was not thankful for others. She always greeted others with a smile while she was busy working in the local hospital or at a church service. She always welcomed others in her life, except for our family dog Max. Aunt Janet was always scared of that dog. Growing up with her in my life, she never appeared to have met a stranger. Her deep regard for anyone, anywhere, truly inspired me to live that way. We lost her in 2015, but I hope to inspire future generations the same way she inspired my generation. I am thankful for her because she is why I can be generous with giving a thank you.

Jessica Provines

Born 1979

Jessica Provines is a psychologist by trade and is Wichita State University through and through. She is currently Assistant Vice President of Wellness and Chief Psychologist at Wichita State University. She goes by many names at work, which include Dr. Provines, Dr. Jess, Jess, and Provines. I go with the last. So, this profile is another special one. She is not just a mentor, not just a friend, but truly an inspiration. She is one of the folks who gave me so many chances to do something special in my career. This relationship starts back during my internship year. I knew we could be friends, but I was just an intern, and she was the training director. During that training year we had little formal interactions. I accepted the job at Wichita State University after my internship year. I was asked by the former director who I wanted to supervise me for my required post-doctoral supervision. I decided to switch things up and work for Dr. Provines to give me another perspective. I would have never thought that decision would have changed my life so much.

What she does is special. I never see her in a meeting where she is not expressing her thanks to everyone involved. Just today I was in a meeting, and she thanked everyone again. It is impressive, but what is even more impressive is that she truly means it. Ultimately, the way she gives her time is what is genuinely amazing. Never in my experience have I seen a leader be willing to put everything else to the side to just be with her staff. She has done it for me so many times and I hope I can continue to pass this on to people I sit with and listen to. She has been a model of a leader who deeply understands the gift of time.

EMBRACE OUR HUMANITY

Let's be clear. You make mistakes, so remember that when your staff members do too. If you just read this last sentence and said to yourself, *I don't make mistakes*, then I am sorry for this, but you are a fool. I will not pull punches with this chapter. If leaders do not think that they make mistakes, they are a part of the problem that so many organizations experience. Leaders who believe they are infallible will always struggle with staff if they think their staff will be unfailing as well. Leaders must embrace their own humanity to see the humanity in their staff.

Thus, one of the most important things to remember is that leadership is love when we embrace our staff's humanity. I ask you to reflect on how life has worked out for you when others recognized your humanity. Think about when someone gave you a break or when they gave you a redo.

Those events are powerful. One moment for me always sticks to my mind. Here you go…

As an undergraduate, I was interviewing for my senior psychology internship placement. I had this interview set up at eight a.m. with the clinic manager at a local mental health clinic. It was the training site I really wanted. So, the morning of the interview I remember waking up to the sound of a shower running. I was thinking, *Why is one of my roommates in the shower this early*? Then I thought to myself, *Why hasn't my alarm gone off yet*? Then I looked at my alarm clock and thought, *Oh shit!* I jumped out of bed, skipped the shower, rushed to get dressed, and found my phone. I called the clinic manager in a panic. I was apologizing while trying to put one leg into my pants. Then the craziest thing happened. He told me to come in a couple of hours later to do the interview. He did not say, "Sorry, next," and move on. He gave me a second chance. I went to the interview later that day. I arrived early. At the end of the interview, I was offered the position and my path continued.

I continue to be grateful to him for giving me a break and recognizing things do not always turn out perfect. It is because of second chances, moments of grace, and goodwill that allows remarkable things to happen. When you have a chance to embrace our humanity, do it. You may never know the impact on someone's life.

Own Mistakes

This part is pretty simple and a challenge for so many leaders.

If you screw up, own it.

This is a message I tell my staff frequently. When they are inexperienced staff members, I say it even more. Why? It is easier to fix a mistake than to hide a mistake. It is easier to take responsibility and move forward than wasting time blaming others or making excuses. As a leader I hold myself to the same standard. You should too.

When leaders own their mistakes, it just makes them more human and creates deeper trust with staff. Mistakes are human, and when you recognize that, your folks will see you more. When they see your flaws and you own them, they will be more likely to own their mistakes.

Additionally, when mistakes happen at work, no matter who does it, the mistake always falls back onto you as the leader. Nothing is more spineless than seeing a leader throw staff under the bus to shield themselves from the blame. I have seen it way too often. I am often embarrassed for the leader who does that, and angered for the staff member who takes the blunt of the fallout from the mistake. Due to this behavior, whenever I have the chance to address this with another leader, I do. I remind them their staff's actions always reflect back on the leader. So, as leaders, they should own the mistake that happened under their watch. They should then work to fix it. I think it is important for leaders to remember that owning mistakes does not mean you made the mistake. It means you take responsibility for it happening. You work to fix the mistake and work to never let it happen again. When we are human, we are more likely to learn from our mistakes.

Be Open to Learning from Your Mistakes

The best thing leaders can take from being human in the workplace is learning from their mistakes. If you truly do not think you make mistakes, then there is so much learning left on the table. Do not be the leader who makes the same mistakes over and over while not attempting to grow from them. If this is because you believe it is a weakness to admit and learn from mistakes, you will struggle to engage in real leadership. Amazing leaders will maintain a curious mindset and always be open to learning from their behaviors, no matter if the outcomes of those actions are positive or negative.

Being human is first knowing that you will make mistakes, and second, being willing to learn from said mistakes.

The rewards from learning from mistakes are many. This learning not only benefits you as a leader down the road, but it can benefit your whole organization. As someone who has learned so much from my mistakes, I have been able to pass down the wisdom. In my roles, I caution others about past projects and ideas that did not work and even gave warnings to staff going down a path mistaken for success. Your learning from mistakes gives others in the organization the opportunity to learn from your mistakes too.

Finally, leaders can take the knowledge gained from a mistake and apply it to the organization to set up the organization for the better. It is always powerful to think about how adversity makes us and others better. When you learn to enjoy challenges and grow from mistakes, it can spread into your workplace. A workplace where they are doing both is destined to succeed.

Do Not Be Stubborn

If you for some reason you think you cannot say you are sorry, do not be stubborn. Stubbornness is another culture killer, especially when it comes from leadership. Stubbornness is a cousin of arrogance. Leadership through arrogance and stubbornness leads only to poor relationships within your organization. Stubbornness is also not the same as persistence. There are many reasons to be persistent as a leader. Do not hide your stubbornness behind the false front of persistence. Doing so just makes a leader look lacking in insight and self-awareness in their interpersonal relationships—which, as I said, is a culture killer. If you have ever worked under a leader without self-awareness or insight, you know first-hand the toll stubborn leaders take on organizations. Staff flight follows, which will then continue to repeat itself.

Say Sorry and Mean It

Saying sorry is easy. Just make sure you mean it. This can be one of the hardest things a leader will do. It can feel exceedingly difficult to say sorry even though it will never hurt you, except possibly your pride. If your pride is hurt, maybe that is a sign that you should work on being humble. When we hurt someone, we should own that, no matter how big or small or how much it impacts our pride. This also does not mean we should live with that impact forever or be guilted by the other person. So, say sorry and repair the relationship. Leading is all about doing hard things and focusing on relationships.

This section might contain one of the hardest things for a leader to do. This is because leaders often hurt a lot of feelings by the nature of our decisions; decisions we control and must take responsibility for. What happens when you lead with love is that you recognize the impact of those choices on your staff. You hear your staff, and you still must make those difficult choices in life.

True leadership is not making everyone happy. It's being willing to listen when you are making individuals unhappy.

But you don't always have to listen to them.

This is a scary moment for some folks reading this book. We are now going to talk about emotions. It is even scarier for people when they talk about their emotions to others. Some leaders even like to declare emotions as not having any place within their organization. That is a naïve way to look at staff and a laughable way to think if you have ever met another human being.

Leaders need to have some emotional intelligence or at least be willing to learn. Leaders need to have empathy. Leaders need to be able to read the room. Sometimes our own emotional response in the workplace can assist leaders in reading the room and developing a response in the moment. It is important that leaders stay in touch with their own emotions. Again, being aware of and feeling emotions—your own and others'—can be beneficial to you and your organization.

That does not mean feeling your emotions will dictate your behavior. But it allows us as leaders to prepare for the impact our decisions will have on staff if you know how you are feeling about your choice. Do not let your emotions be your only guide in relationships. Missteps happen when leaders forget to look at the whole picture and see the view from above.

Sometimes a leader's feelings are off compared to reality. For instance, I had to make a rough decision in the office—I was preparing for the challenge of telling a staff member they would have to continue in a role I believed they would feel isolated in. I spoke with a leadership team member about how I did not like this choice, but it was the right choice to best serve everyone involved. The leadership team member agreed. So, I met with the staff member one-on-one and let them know of the plan and how this role of theirs would continue, likely for a minimum of another year.

To my surprise, they were not as emotionally stressed as I expected. They were comfortable with this setup continuing because it allowed them to be closer to their children's daycare and gave them more time alone to stay on top of notes. The moral of the story for me was that sometimes your emotions do not match the emotions of the staff members you are leading.

Now, for another word of caution for leaders. Recognizing your emotions in your organization is imperative regarding avoiding favoritism. I believe leaders can have a personal relationship with staff and should when practicing leadership as love. It can really be a beautiful thing. And leaders must still recognize when those relationships and feelings may be impacting decisions. It becomes inappropriate when leaders include or exclude someone when they like them more or less. This leadership is not treating the staff member you like more better than your other staff you may not like as much. When leadership is love, you are not treating your staff like you are all best friends either.

When a leader's favoritism is in their staff members' faces, a leader's creditability diminishes. For example, I witnessed a room of employees' shock during an event where the leader picked a staff member to choose one of the few giveaway items after the staff member complimented their leadership. The moment felt ridiculous for me, and I saw that I was not alone. This moment highlights, for me as a leader, how leaning into your emotions can end poorly and you not even realize.

Hence, there are three points to remember about feeling your emotions. First, be in touch with your emotions and how they may be pulling you in a certain direction. Second, do not assume your emotional reactions will always be the same as your employees. Lastly, do not allow your emotions to stop important decisions from happening. Letting your emotions guide you could be a mistake when there is a chance you could be allowing emotions to mislead your decisions.

Staff Emotions First

Do not let embracing your humanity become an excuse to monopolize emotions in your office. Like I have laid out the importance of feeling your emotions, I implore you to never let your emotions be the theme in the office nor the focus of meetings when your staff need their feelings heard first.

Leaders are welcome to have meetings where they lead off discussing their frustrations or worries with employees. Leaders should feel welcome to discuss their reactions to statements from staff or events within or outside the workplace and the impact on them or their staff. It can be helpful when employees know where their leaders stand emotionally on things impacting the staff. Again, it helps leaders to embrace our humanity and build that meaningful relationship within the workplace with staff. Having emotions and hearing staff emotions can deepen those relationships.

The problem leaders can have is when they take over the emotion in the room. This can make staff feel pressured to manage the leaders' feelings. I caution leaders all the time about taking up too much emotional space in the office. The staff's role is not about managing a leader's feelings. Your job is about making more space for your staff's emotions, not taking away that space from them.

Remember Your Humanity

I will end on this note for the chapter: Remember your humanity when you make decisions. Lean into this to help you understand others better in the office. When you must make tough decisions that impact individuals negatively, remember how you would want to be treated. More importantly, if you have built your relationships with staff members, remember how they would want to be treated. Then treat them that way! It will make a difference in the long run. Treating them with empathy and humanity will not change the tough decisions that need to be made. It will change, however, the experience for you and the staff during those challenging times.

Remember—be caring, be kind, and embrace our humanity.

EMBRACE OUR HUMANITY

Profiles of Inspiration

Stefani Hathaway

Born 1977

Stefani Hathaway earned her doctorate in counseling psychology from the University of Missouri-Columbia in 2005, after which she joined the Bowling Green State University counseling center that same year. I was fortunate our paths crossed in 2017. I became the Assistant Director/Clinical Director at Bowling Green. She was a more senior psychologist, and I was now her supervisor. I was nervous because she had been practicing for ten years more than I had. I came in believing the most important thing I would be learning from her was clinically related. However, she helped me truly see being human in supervisory relationships. Because of this experience, our supervisory relationship is one of my most cherished experiences in my career.

The humility she radiated and grace she gave me and others on staff continue to be second to none. During that single year I was there she modeled a willingness to own mistakes, grow from them, and be flexible more than some of the people I have known for years. After I left in the summer of 2018, Stefani then became the Assistant Director. I knew she was nervous about taking on that new role, but it was one I completely believed she could do if she stayed herself. We still keep in touch from time to time, and every time I see her name pop up on my phone a smile radiates from my face.

Chukwunenye Nweke

Born 1995

Chukwunenye "Chuck" Nweke was born and raised in Nigeria. In 2014, he traveled to the United States to attend college at Emporia State University in Kansas. Chuck completed his clinical internship at Wichita State University during the 2021–2022 school year while enrolled in his master's program at Emporia State. This is how I met him. During that year, I had the pleasure of clinically supervising Chuck. In our weekly supervision I got to learn so much about him. I got to learn about his deep belief in family, his joy in relationships, and his openness to learning.

Who I met that year as a supervisee was someone with extremely limited clinical experience, but also someone who is extremely open to learning. After that year together, we were able to keep him on staff. To this day, I am thankful for his ability to own his mistakes and make things right. What I appreciate most about my time with Chuck is he allowed me into his world. It has increased my own growth, pushed me more as a supervisor, and made me a better human.

DREAM BIGGER FOR OTHERS

"Ad Astra Per Aspera"

In Kansas, this is the state moto. It means "To the stars through difficulties." In Kansas, you often see *Ad Astra* printed on merchandise in local shops, as themes at local and state level conferences, in business names, and mentioned in many speeches. Those words mean so much more than lip service to the locals, and capture the Kansan entrepreneurial spirit well. Life is about reaching for big dreams, and way too often our difficulties stop us. As a leader, I want to find out what my staff's "stars" are to them. I want to find out their dreams and goals. As a leader you want to create an environment that allows them to travel beyond their dreams and goals. You want them to reach beyond the stars and move through the challenges of work and the difficulties of life. Truly allowing them to be their best selves.

Work with your employees to dream together and envision a future of success. When you create opportunities within your organization to bring staff together, make it meaningful. Do not let those retreats, staff building events, or feedback meetings be in vain. Make those times that already happen, or create separate times within your organizations, to dream, develop, and reflect. Employees that see their future can see what they need to do to grow.

Sometimes big dreams do not include you or your organization, which is okay. A leader's goal is to help their staff move forward, not hold them back. If their future includes you, great. If it does not, your goals as a leader for them still do not change. If this job is a launching point, help them launch. If their goal is a long-term career within your organization, help them succeed. You might be surprised when they come back. Why they come back might surprise you more. It is likely because you supported them and helped them grow.

Finally, one of the greatest things as a leader you can witness is when you see your staff members reach the stars. You get to look back with joy, knowing they allowed you to be a part of their journey.

People Are Always More Capable Than We Give Them Credit

People often receive messages that silence their dream. It can be outwardly received, or internal thoughts that are reinforced by others or ourselves. Leaders create possibilities for staff. They might not see it in themselves, but it is in them. Leadership is love creates the possibility for staff to dream again.

An experience I had as a supervisor really highlights the importance of believing in staff more than they believe in themselves. When I was a clinical director, I had a therapist who was overwhelmed because of the amount of work they had regarding their client caseload. They stated their prior supervisor would just lighten the caseload because the therapist thought it was too much for them to handle.

I challenged that idea.

I let the therapist know how I felt the supervisor let them down. That supervisor did not see any greater ability in that therapist, but I knew there was from their other clinical work. Then, there was a face of surprise when I told the therapist my thoughts. I think there was even some shock. But I meant it. I truly did! Our goal as leaders should be to always help make our staff better. We should not be holding employees back based on their own reservations. Leaders help staff work through their self-doubt. Leaders should be able to help staff see beyond their own horizon.

So, believe in folks more than they believe in themselves. No one is ever a finished product when they start a job or start learning something new.

We should never treat individuals as if they are done.

When we do, people will travel only the distance they believe they can go. Individuals are always capable of a greater distance. A leader's role is to help staff see the possibilities and then pave the roads when staff start moving beyond their horizon.

DREAM BIGGER FOR OTHERS

Profiles of Inspiration

Melissa Leonard

Born 1985

Melissa, or "Missy" to me, is as you have guessed, my wife. We met in high school, my sophomore year. It was one of those cute love stories where we met in class, flirted, and we would cruise around the Illinois Valley while secretly liking each other without telling the other. We then started dating my junior year. From then on, our love story wrote itself.

Missy has always inspired me. Whether it be her love of others, selflessness, or belief in others, she is always giving. What makes me lucky in my life is my wife. It is because of her that this all happened to me. She believed in me more than I have ever believed in myself.

Now, it is not that I did not work hard to get here today, but this journey is an emotional rollercoaster for so many individuals. Missy was the one who held on for the whole ride. The emotional strength she had to hold our relationship and family together is a miracle. And what astonishes me more is that during the craziness of graduate school, moving, and raising children, she always believed I could do more and make a difference. That is the power of dreaming bigger for others; she helped me see where I could go.

She was the one who encouraged me to take risks, apply for jobs, move, dream bigger, and be bold. All the while, Missy knew how these dreams would change our lives for the better. And she knew the challenges that come with big dreams. She accepted the risks of failure, but she supported me throughout this journey because she saw more in me than I saw at that time.

IT'S THE RELATIONSHIP, STUPID

As Part II wraps up, you have probably realized the underlying theme of all successful leadership:

It's the relationship, stupid!

It is weird to think that I would reference the political strategist James Carville from the 1990s, but I really do not think there is anything that sums leadership up better. The heart of leadership is the relationship. Power and authority can get individuals to run at walls. The power of the relationship is what gets them to run through the wall. When you create true relationships with your people, the possibilities are endless in what they can or are willing to do for your organization's mission and, more importantly, for each other.

As a psychologist, I have learned so much about the importance of the relationship in therapy. However, I will share with you the hesitation I had when I started out in my graduate training. Back during graduate school, I kept thinking that I needed to learn all these technical skills, theoretical orientations, and clinical interventions. I was not wrong—those are extremely important. Nevertheless, throughout my training we learned the importance of the therapeutic relationship and how it accounts most for the change in client outcomes.

Yes, I said it. In therapy, the most important thing is the relationship. Who works with you as the therapist, their orientation, and their level of training are not as important as the relationship created between the individuals in the therapy room. So, why am I talking so much about psychology right here when the book is about leadership? The field of psychology focuses on human behavior. As a leader, the majority of what you do as a manager is focused on human behavior. The connection has always been clear to me. Leadership is really all about psychology.

Now, a word of caution related to my hesitation to focus on relationships mainly in graduate school. New staff and new leaders often fall into the trap of thinking their job is doing something correctly and need the tool or technique to make this happen. They lose sight of the customer or staff member in front of them. This error not only costs the leader and staff member growth, connection, and success, the person in front of them loses the most and experiences the biggest disconnect from the organization to which they devoted their time.

So yes, as leaders your main job with your staff is focusing on relationships and seeing the culture build right in front of you. Once you do that, the rest of the work can begin. You can learn then about the real needs of your staff. Foster the environment and culture that breeds success for your field and watch your staff shine. Helping your staff shine will lead only to the company shining brighter.

This is how leadership is love.

Hard things are not easy.

That is what makes you different.

...which one are you?

PART III

The Practical

Like getting a horse to drink water, control of employees is an illusion. You can, however, create the environment for them to want to drink.

Do they drink to a toast or because they are parched?

RECOGNIZE THE LUCK

There are so many choices we can make in life. Many times, we act on autopilot and do not realize how one choice can change the whole trajectory of our life. We think benign choices do not matter, but the impact will be seen down the road. It is to me the butterfly effect of our lives. As we begin Part III, I wanted to share a particular lucky moment for me.

A light bulb memory of my luck was when it came to making choices regarding my doctoral internship site-selection process. I was planning to go to a training site in Wichita, Kansas. Then during the semester as I was applying to internship sites, I got excited about providing clinical supervision. I found myself providing supervision to other trainees at my graduate program while I was taking a class on clinical supervision. I decided I wanted to continue my training. So, I went back to my site-selection list to review my options. It was my good old Excel sheet list, a list I started my first year of graduate school and revised every year. I liked this one site in Wichita, but that particular site did not have the supervision opportunity I was seeking for the following year. In that moment, I decided to change to the other site in Wichita that allowed me to further develop and train in providing supervision. That site ended up being Wichita State University Counseling and Psychological Services (Counseling and Testing Center at the time).

Here is the funny thing about luck. A month or so later, during the interview phase, the original site I wanted to apply for pulled out of being an internship site the following year. If I had stayed with that first site, I would not be in Wichita writing this book, raising my kids, or being a part of this special workplace. I look back on that moment when I switched sites and always smile and think about all those what ifs. The space I am in today started because of a minor change on an Excel sheet on my computer. It is just that wild! I see the luck.

Are your eyes open to see your luck?

Beyond choices, I also see the importance of timing. Looking at the big picture gives me perspective. Seeing the luck of timing allows me to recognize how the time and place in which I grew up gave me so many more opportunities than others have experienced. Luck with timing, such as how after my internship year in Wichita they were hiring psychologists at my site. So many years, I see new trainees leave because there are no open positions at my workplace. I am lucky there was one when I graduated. Position openings always have so much to do with timing and luck. As leaders, we all need to remember our luck with timing. Still, we do not get to leadership positions without hard work and persistence. Trust-fund babies and keys-to-the-company kids might be the exceptions, but that still can be a misconception because I have never been in their shoes, so I will give them some grace.

One reason we as leaders need to see our luck is because this awareness colors how we interact with our staff. When we pretend our success is only because of our hard work and persistence, we end up lying to our staff. This lie then becomes counterproductive in the moment, and in the long run, with our staff. Worst of all, as leaders you might start to believe the lie. Anything worth doing is never done alone, or without something going our way—a bit of luck. Leaders who act with gratitude recognize their luck and everything that got them to where they are today.

Leaders who do not recognize their luck sound very out of touch. Staff will lose respect for those leaders, especially when leaders think they hit a triple, but actually started on second base. Thus, leaders who are trying to create a productive and healthy culture cannot be the only one in the room that does not recognize their luck. Staying with the baseball metaphor, you will be behind in the count. So, from the start of your career, leadership, or relationships, own your luck and your hard work.

REALIZE WHAT MATTERS TO THEM MATTERS TO YOU

Show that You Care

For so many leaders, the concepts in this chapter will make or break a lot of teams within an organization. Leaders need to let their staff see that they do not just talk like they care about their staff, but show they do care. A leader's relationship with staff only strengthens when they know the relationship is genuine. Leaders often show interest in their staff's interests and personal lives. However, is this interest just a front? Is this just a trick that leaders use to make their staff think they care? This is a moment for honest reflection. Do you genuinely care about your staff? Do you really want to know about their weekend? When your leadership is love, your answer is a loud...

Yes!

Now, what I like to say is that this does not mean you have to be passionate about what they do or like. That would be ingenuine if you pretend to be passionate when you are not. Judgement may be more authentic, but this is about empathy and enjoying the fact that those unique things bring joy and meaning to your staff. And I receive joy from hearing about my staff members' weekend and the joy that it brought them. Yet, the content of the weekend is not as important as the emotional experience from the weekend. This is when I am super authentic with staff about their passions.

For instance, I love hearing about wonderful experiences at seafood or sushi restaurants and what my staff ate. How they talk about their experiences matters to me. Then I follow up with how happy I am that they enjoyed their sushi or seafood and how I would never eat that. They laugh back because they know I am a basic steak and potato guy. The point, however, is that I know the joy of an amazing steak. If they loved their meal as much as I loved that steak, then they had an amazing meal. And that is the essence of their experience and this chapter. What matters to them should matter to you because they will experience joy and pain in their lives just as you have. Thus, you connect with them on how it feels, no matter the topic, content, or experience. This always gives leaders some things to engage in with staff and connect to their humanity.

Go See Them in Public

This is one of the straightforward things a leader can do when they really care about what matters to staff. See them outside of the office. If they have something going on and they invite you, go, make an appearance. See them thrive outside of the workplace. Meet their family and extended family at gatherings. Truly show you care about what brings them joy and makes them happy.

For instance, one time I had a staff member who was interested in taking on acrobatic exercise and performance. She was always talking about it and over lunch even showed the bruises from the challenging nature of the acrobatics. This staff member had an upcoming performance at a medieval fair in the local area. Now, my family and I have no real interest in medieval fairs. I have heard of them, was a little curious, and a family member of mine might have even been in one in the past. Still, it is just not one of the regular things my family and I did, but I knew the staff member was excited to perform. This is where connecting to what is important to staff matters. So, we carved out some time in our weekend and saw the performance. Let me just say, the routine was pretty impressive, and my family and I had a splendid time checking out the rest of the fair. The staff member was appreciative of us coming to see them perform, but I was truly more appreciative of the staff member sharing her joy with me, the other staff, and my family.

Empathize with Joy and Loss

As I have said earlier in this chapter, empathy means being a leader who recognizes what matters to their staff matters to them. You do not even need to like it, but understanding why it matters to them always helps you learn more about their joy and their pain.

Sharing in joy is one of the best things you can do in the workplace. For the past couple of years, several staff members have been big Taylor Swift fans. They talk about saving money to go to concerts. One even traveled to another country to see her perform during her Eras Tour. I will be frank, I do not really care that much for her music, but this is not the book for that discussion. Nonetheless, their joy that comes from her music and the connection other staff members have to each other from her music is awesome. When I speak to them about their connection to her music, I go to my connection. The band I love is the Red Hot Chili Peppers. They are a band I have followed since the mid-1990s. I have been to a respectable number of shows and know firsthand how joyful music concerts and music can be for individuals. As a leader, I tap into that joy I experience when discussing music with the Swifties in the office. I do this instead of shutting down conversations in the workplace about things in my staff's lives.

I would rather connect with staff than dismiss them.

When I hear about workers' pain in the workplace, a lack of empathy is one of the hardest things I have witnessed or read about. However, when leaders can identify with the feelings of their staff members, they can make a world of difference. For instance, I get disappointed when I read articles and see the lack of empathy in the reactions to a person's bereavement regarding a loss of a pet. I have had to put down pets in the past and still did not take time off. I also have lost family members and have taken time off. If I were told I could not take time off for a loss of a pet and I had the same emotional response as a loss of a family member, I would likely quit. I have had staff who have taken more time off for loss of a pet than other staff members take off for relatives who pass. If that relationship is that deep and meaningful, hopefully like other relationships in your life, why would I not appreciate the importance of that relationship in the staff member's life?

Ultimately, your ability to lead improves when you have empathy for those under your leadership. Connect with them, show them you care about what is important to them, and see them give that same or greater level of empathy to you and your clientele. More empathy does not just improve your relationships within the workplace, empathy improves our communities, culture, and undoubtedly the world.

ENJOY CHALLENGES

This is the work. We face challenges everyday as leaders. When you lead people, be ready for them to bring their problems and their conflicts to work, as well as their annoyance with co-workers' behaviors. Leaders always face challenges in what we do, create, or provide in our work. This aspect of our work is usually accepted. However, I feel when leaders talk about work issues with personnel, they complain. That always surprises me because issues with personnel are also the work. Our people are the work. They always have been the work. Leadership is never easy, so as I said—"Enjoy the challenges."

Be Ready to Be Uncomfortable

Work always comes with challenges and change comes from discomfort. So, the easiest thing I think we can do is to embrace change and challenges. Embrace the growing pains. Accept progress. Nothing recently captures change and challenges like COVID-19. People have many reactions when thinking about the early 2020s during the height of COVID-19. This pandemic also elevated how we work in my office to new heights. That would not have happened within five years if the pandemic had not started in 2020.

While at Wichita State University in March 2020, we were told we were going remote for two weeks. Our department aimed to go remote and have no interruption in therapy services. In that ever-changing time, we shifted to remote work without any gaps in our clinical services. That meant our office closed Friday and we went home. Monday morning, we opened right back up at eight a.m., but remotely. Was that a heavy lift…

You bet it was!

The goals we had in our office would not change. We just had to figure out a way to do this. The good news was, if your clinicians are therapeutically sound, your center just needs to be trained on how to do it online instead of in-person. So, in the time leading up to going remote, our office had a lot to do. Our office trained the clinicians for remote work. We procured proper security and staff laptops for clinical work. The clinical leadership team then engaged in advanced training for remote clinical operations. On top of that, all trainees were pulled back from their training year, which left the office short staffed. However, through that discomfort, our office and staff grew together and stronger.

Throughout being remote during COVID-19, additional challenges arose. We had to upgrade our electronic medical record functions and change our billing process. Our office did all this while maintaining quality services. This experience and change are where I really found so much of my leadership. It was during this time I realized that I not only enjoy challenges, but I also seek them out. I thanked a trusted colleague for pointing that out to me.

Now, for the leaders who do not like challenges as I do, I am sorry to tell you, but challenges will never go away. It is our duty to learn how to manage our discomfort and embrace such challenges. So, for our challenge-weary leaders, what can you do? Simply accept that change and challenges are constant, remember challenges are not reflections of poor leadership, and engage in supportive behaviors when distress becomes overwhelming.

Verbal Challenges

Leadership is hardly black or white. We need to live in the grey. People who work for us are too many tones and shades to be treated with binary policies. For example, you will read later about empowered employees. You will learn about how when leaders have empowered workers, they will challenge you more. This is good. So again, enjoy challenges.

You also need to allow yourself as a leader to be challenged. This is critical for your success. It makes you, your office, and your staff better. When you take on the mindset that being challenged is good, the easier it becomes to hear it. The more open you are to hearing challenges, the better your staff will be open to challenging you. Again, the better you are at enjoying challenges, the better your organization will run.

Challenges today will lead to growth tomorrow.

Smell the Roses

I firmly believe this is difficult and demanding work, and much of the hard work is enjoyable when you see that you got through the discomfort. I also believe you can smell the roses during the challenges too. Again, often the complaint about the role of a leader or manager is dealing with people problems and if we could just focus on the product, customer, you name it, the job would be fine.

The reality is your job as a leader and manager is to work with your staff's issues. Your workers focus on the organization's customer, product, or service. You focus on them, address their needs, and enjoy the process as it unfolds in front of you. You help them face their challenges in the workplace. Enjoy the process and you will see the growth of your staff. This is where, as leaders, we can dream bigger for them. We can see the future in front of them, if they are willing to face those challenges with you. You will get to look back on the challenges you and your organization faced and realize you got through it. That is a truth about challenges. Often only after we get through the challenge do we breathe. I encourage more from leaders in these times. Leaders ought to inhale and smell the roses *during* the challenge and *during* the process of dealing with it.

I will end this chapter with a quote from a former university president at Wichita State University, Dr. John Bardo. He led transformational change at WSU, and he would speak about the challenges. What he would state is something I have adopted with a close mentor of mine during periods of fast-paced change and turbulence. It is a reminder that our duty as leaders is not only to face challenges, but in reality, facing challenges is a part of our work.

Isn't this fun?

USE A DATA-INFORMED MINDSET

What is a Data-Informed Mindset?

Well, being data informed means collecting all the data you can get while also listening to your own and your employee's experiences to make wise decisions. It is taking in all the data points you can collect while keeping the human experience in mind. Why would this book about how leadership is love have a chapter on data? That's easy—data is helpful. Data supports our curiosity and strengthens our next steps. So many cultures, companies, and organizations are data driven. However, leadership is more than being data driven. It matters so much more to be data informed than data driven.

Organizations that are data driven shy away from wisdom, risk, innovation, and humanity in the office. A data-driven mentality is the opposite of being data informed. Do not become the leaders who lose the humanity, the experience, the heart, and the wisdom of our work and workplace. Leaders who are data informed can see how the hard data and experience of the staff may be incongruent. The leader then can respond with love and curiosity instead of telling staff they are underperforming, or there is no reason to be stressed because this is not even a peak season for their company.

Being data informed allows leaders to make choices with data in mind, not blindly following what the data states. It allows leaders to use their humanity when the data and experience do not match. It allows leaders to support and use wisdom rather than treating staff as company cogs.

As a leader myself, I have leaned into data more than any of the prior leaders in my role. Data has saved me more times than not. Yet, I still know the limits of data. With that in mind, leaders should seek both to know and understand data holistically to fully see leadership as love.

If we are going to keep data...

Why Not Do It Well?

Very often we need to track some aspect of what we do or lead. If you are not tracking, please start. When we set up ourselves and our data with the understanding of how it will be seen, used, or interpreted, do it right from the start.

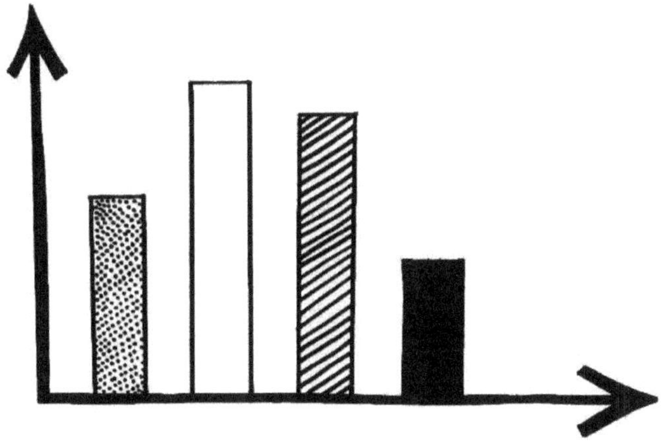

The old saying "measure twice, cut once" rings too true in this area. If leaders collect wrong data, measure wrong, use only metrics as guides, or do not measure at all, they set themselves up for extra work and truly little reward. Worst of all, when people below you see how the data in your organization is meaningless, not used, or wrong, their morale regarding data collection goes down. Make their data meaningful and in turn they will see their work as meaningful as well.

Why Not Be Data Informed?

Now that you think I love data, let me clear the air. I do not! The hairs on the back of my neck stand up whenever I hear "data driven."

We should always be people-and-relationship-driven.

Data should be viewed as an important part of the story. However, it is never the whole story. Let me say that again. Data is never the whole story. Data gives us a starting point to ask questions. Sometimes it even answers a question, but data does not make the decision of what to do next.

You do!

As the leader with the data, you get to see the whole picture when you include all the other pieces. Leadership can also see those pieces of the organization that cannot be quantified. It is the feelings leaders know and hear but cannot write down. Additionally, there is the gut and wisdom data that come from experience. Those are the data points you cannot disregard, ever. I genuinely think all data should be reviewed. Leaders and organizations should always be seeking meaning. True meaning can be understood only when data is allowed in all forms.

Strive to Make Your Data Impressive

So now you know that I am not in love with data, and yet I still see the utility of having data. Leaders must accept that data will forever be a part of leadership. Hence, leaders should strive to do data well. I was reading a news article a long time ago and the athletic director at the University of Alabama at the time was quoted saying something to the effect of…

"If you are going to keep score, you might as well try to win."

That statement has aways stuck out to me when I think about data. When leaders are collecting data, make sure to make it impressive. Like I have stated earlier, make it meaningful. Give your data legs. Do not collect data on nonsense in the office. When you do collect it, make sure you collect it for a while. Do not change how you collect data on certain things every year. You will never be able to really assess trends, patterns, or problems if you are always changing your method of data collection.

A great test for the value of your data is a simple reflection. Is your data boring? Are you glossing over it when reviewing? If you as a leader experience this when reviewing your own data, then you have a problem. To address this, reflect on your data. Does the data tell your story, expand understanding, or push your organization forward? When leaders are bored, the data is likely not doing any of the three.

As leaders, you can push the organization to do a better job with the data. With a data-informed mindset, you cannot just tell the story better, but you will know the story. Leaders can take in all the data and expand their understanding of the customer, product, service, and organization. Finally, this mindset allows all leaders to act boldly, see the whole picture, and guide the organization into the future.

This might seem like a long chapter for someone who stated they do not like data so much. With such a focus on relationships in the workplace, why so much again on data? Well, it is clear to me from the start, every relationship is filled with data points. Are you willing to see them and reflect on what they are telling you as a leader?

SIGNAL YOUR TEAM

What is your signal to your team? "Do epic shit" is mine. But, before I tell you more about this, we should start at the beginning. For a long time, I have found that concise, yet meaningful messages impact others. Words and images matter. When we see the success of chants, traditions, and colors in the sporting world, it helps players and fans recognize they are a part of something bigger than themselves. That is the importance of a signal. What makes signals work even better is when they are unique to your organization. If it is a buzzword or a term another company is using, why would your employees not just work for them? Your organization does not stand out when the leaders talk about priorities in the same way other organizations do. The impact will be lost.

Leaders need a meaningful, unique, and powerful signal.

Kick-Ass

My signal started with the endearing term: Kick-Ass. Why the hyphen? It started from a presentation I went to earlier in my career. The presenter asked us to come up with one word to decide our purpose. Me, being a little rebellious and one who does not like to follow the rules, I added the hyphen so I could have my one word. From that day on and for over the next four years, Kick-Ass was my term. I used it to describe how I felt, the actions I would take, as well as how I planned for others to act.

Kick-Ass then became the simple signal to describe the energy and tenacity of us at the counseling center. During those four years, I could not help but notice that the department *was* kicking ass. Still, the signal did not capture where our culture in the department was going. We were moving away from just excelling at the work we were doing. The group needed a new signal to guide our culture into our next phase. So, I introduced the concept of DES. You might ask, "What does DES mean?" It means not accepting the status quo, not doing things "bush league," and working to bring change and make a true difference for yourself and others in this world. It means...

Do Epic Shit

Say what you will, but I am unapologetic about this signal and its meaning. I am also unapologetic about wanting things to change for the better. So, I brought this concept into the office to start the next phase. Staff attached to the message and aligned with the concept. Then we, as an office, had fun integrating DES into the culture at work. We created stickers to solidify this as our signal and symbol. Though, these stickers could only be earned once the employee exhibited behaviors that align with DES. To make this even better, this is a pretty epic sticker that was created by a staff member who was excited about rolling out DES in the office.

The idea behind these signals is that with a clear simple message, individuals will join together and become a team. They will gain pride in being a part of something bigger than themselves. You see this all around with individuals who show immense pride in groups and organizations. They feel a sense of belonging and these symbols represent their connection. As stated earlier, symbols matter, and universities and professional sports teams nail this. Your workplace should take note. Powerful organizations make signals a part of their DNA. Those organizations do not treat their signals as just lip service. Those organizations' team members can end up attacking and changing anything in front of them. It is very impressive when leaders can create purpose and develop a signal to expand that purpose. Those teams are always moving at a faster pace than any other group around them.

Give a team a clear purpose with an impactful message and watch them give it their all.

SET UP YOUR CHESSBOARD

Set up your team like you would set up a chessboard. Get the right people on the board in the right roles. Leaders want the right people on the board, respecting each other and working together toward the same goal. Those are the people your organization wants to employ. Once you have those individuals at your workplace, your organization will be able to move strategically, striking at the right time together. Setting up the board right allows all parties to see the role they play and how important their role is in accomplishing the organization's purpose.

Now, there may be some folks working against a positive work culture at your organization. Your job as a leader with those employees is twofold. First, leaders need to be curious about why their employee is working against the office culture. Second, you help them find an exit strategy and you let them set their course. The second point is one that took a while for me to grasp as a leader, but it is important to remember.

Why would you keep unhappy folks?!

Remember you want what is best for them and what is best for the culture at your organization. Leadership is love is not about abandoning staff. This is not about spite. It is about being honest about timing, fit, and goals. I genuinely believe that everyone can be on the board. It just might not work at this time if the fit, goals, and timing are off. Therefore, it means they might not thrive in your culture right now. That is okay. This is especially important for leaders to hear who try to make everyone happy at every moment. Additionally, while we are on the topic of unhappy staff, remember if everyone is unhappy in your culture, what is going on with your culture? Go back to step one and get feedback to make changes.

Build Your Board

Invest in your team first and always. Leaders will find out quickly who on their team wants to go in the same direction. This also helps you learn who does not want to leave the comfort of the status quo, and sadly, those who want to go in a different direction. Having curious conversations with these last two groups of employees help leaders learn how to move forward with them.

Investing in your teams allows leaders to see how much the staff members invest back into the company. Lean into those members and help them see their role on the board. Help them see how their role contributes to the bigger picture and where their future is within the company. Building the board is always a chance for leaders to dream bigger for their staff. Lead with love and help them dream.

Now, when your team members have the same desire and purpose and see the direction in which the company is heading, the strength of the organization builds. The strength of your culture is reinforced. When the process of deciding how to get there is made and everyone is on board, what comes next is the truest test of investment, engagement, and trust of the culture or team.

Is Your Staff Improving or Static?

Does your staff want to get better? Do they see that their growth benefits both them and the organization? What you see from these behaviors tells you a lot about how they view their work and role within the organization. Leaders know they have a strong growth-focused organization when they feel they must pump the brakes versus having to motivate their staff to engage in growth.

Realize, leaders always need to focus on building their team. Your team members are the future of the organization. Know that your organization's future can start at any time. Every time a leader has a new goal, they can set up their board again. Get the right people on the board now and find out how much everyone will enjoy moving forward.

CHOOSE PEOPLE OVER WORK

Choosing people over work is essential to me as a leader. Work will always be there, your people will not. I have often thought about what a work week would look like if I showed up, shut my door, and did everything on my task list. However, I remind myself of two truths in my job:

1. There will always be more work next week.

2. Being available to staff and staff relationships are tasks too.

I just never put number two on my to-do list at work. For me, it would be like me having a reminder to put on a seatbelt. At this point, wearing a seatbelt is second nature for me. Still, cars have the seatbelt chime for folks whom wearing a seatbelt is not second nature. Let's say that this book is your beep.

When we structurally set ourselves up to exclude relationships in the office, we lose the heart and love that is needed in leadership. Leaders are avoiding their humanity in the workplace. Do not let fears of relationships exclude you from choosing people over work. Leadership is love because we move away from fears in our leadership.

Now realize, this does not mean I never close my door, but when I do, I am aware of the potential costs to the organization. This often leads to me never shutting the door because regularly the other left work waiting costs less than losing relationships in the office.

Work cultures are fragile.

Leaders must constantly be aware and nurture their workplace culture. Choosing relationships over work helps leaders feed their culture. Sometimes, and likely more often than not, this will cost leaders time on their individual tasks. This is the choice of the leader to make. But as I have said, managing relationships in the organization is the leader's job.

I know what choices I have made. Do you?

CREATE AN EXPERIENCE

Your staff are not cogs in a machine. If they were, you would not need leaders or managers. You would just need maintenance and information technology staff. Since staff are not cogs, they will always have options for other workplaces or opportunities within or outside your sector. So, as leaders we need to be competitive with other job opportunities. This is not about putting a slide in the office or making your workplace a gimmick. You could put a slide in the office if you really wanted it, but it must be about creating a holistic experience within the workplace that meets your staff's desires. Yes, I said desires. We want folks to want to come to work. We want folks to enjoy their time off but also miss some aspects of the work too. Why would an employee ever miss work? It is simple...

Relationships and experiences!

When you create experiences through relationships, there is a desire to be a part of something. When people realize their experiences add to their growth or make a greater change in this world, their desire increases. Now, people can work in fields because of their desire. We see that all the time in higher education. However, upon working within the field, the desire might wane. Why? Well, my hypothesis is that desire wanes because of poor experiences at work. Did they not get what they needed? Was their desire not fed with experiences that aligned with their values and goals? Right! This matters.

Create an experience at your organization that matters to your people.

Let's Talk About Money

Leaders seem to think that people do not like talking about money with employees. I do. I actually do a lot, for one straightforward reason. Money matters to my employees. I believe it matters to the overwhelming majority of employees. If it does not, then the employee is naïve or set in life. So, why do I mention money in a chapter about creating experiences?

It is clear. You must give experiences in your workplace a chance. Leaders cannot describe their workplace through an experience lens and attract and retain talent if the company is underpaying employees compared to the market. I lost at least one staff member a year for four years because the pay could never keep up. I never had a chance, even with the culture being created in the office.

I am not asking to lead the market in pay. It would be nice, but I am also realistic. But the best work experience will not keep talent when they can make 40K more a year working less, somewhere else.

Give me a chance!

Honestly, salaries need to be competitive if you want work experiences to matter. As I stated before, employees bring their whole self into work. The whole self includes debts, medical bills, child rearing, and caring for other family members as just a start. When you increase your salaries to be competitive, work experiences will win out and your retention of staff will increase and grow. My office does not lead the market, but we have not lost a staff member in more than two years now. Why?

Money matters, and experiences are why they stay.

Money Goes Only So Far

Yes, money matters. If you do not make your pay competitive your experience will not matter. Additionally, you cannot pay your way out of a terrible experience in a workplace. Eventually those individuals will leave. Your workplace will be stagnant. Staff turnover will become like a revolving door. This is because the people filling those positions behind exited employees will leave soon too.

Don't Be a Slide

Make sure as a leader that your employees' experiences matter. Be in touch with what matters to your staff. An experience where folks get shirts instead of time off matters. People might like treats versus cards. Employees might enjoy personal agency in their jobs versus gifts. Do not be gimmicky. It may be fun to look at a company with a slide in the main office area, but does that matter to your employees? In the end, if it does not matter to your staff, your intention just became a gimmick.

Don't be a slide.

ALLOW PEOPLE TO LET YOU DOWN

The Reality of Humanity

People will let you down, and that is okay. The sooner leaders understand this, the better leaders will be equipped to handle those moments when they happen. Take for instance, meaningful relationships in your life. Have you ever been in a meaningful relationship where the other person did not let you down at least once?

I love my spouse, my kids, my parents, grandparents, and siblings. Trust me, I have been let down before. However, they are still the most important people in my life. I also know I have let them all down too. That is the reality of humanity.

People are not perfect.

The most important thing I take from this is that when you have the right people on your chessboard, you both learn from the mistakes that led to you being let down. Learning from mistakes is at the heart of accepting people letting you down. When both parties involved experience growth and learn from mistakes, what more could you want? It is only human to be let down; it creates a wonderful opportunity to open our hearts up to curiosity and learn together. Having the right people in your workplace turns mistakes into moments where everyone in the organization improves.

Leaders turn disappointments into opportunities for their staff to do better.

Accurate Expectations

So why do you have impossible expectations for staff when you do not have that for family? It is likely because of love. Love with family is often unconditional. Unconditional love at work is a lie. That is why I will never say, "We are one big family here!"

The truth is we have conditions for work. Leaders should not pretend we do not have conditions at work. Still, a belief leaders should have for most work is that perfection at every moment is not possible. Do not pretend that allowing staff to let you down is an excuse for low standards. Leaders must always have standards. Your staff must learn from not meeting those standards. Leadership is love because we hold them to those standards.

Standards are a leader's friend. However, leaders must not sweat the small mistakes, teach what can be learned, and move on. It is easier on everyone. Leaders who make a big deal out of small issues waste everyone's time and energy as well as demoralize staff. Micromanaging and nitpicking are behaviors covering for a leader's fear and trust issues. Do not use "standards" as an excuse to not confront one's fear or inability to trust in the workplace. Leadership as love helps leaders sit with staff member mistakes and focuses on helping them grow from the mistake rather than prevent the issue from ever happening.

Thus, expect the best and allow them to fail at times. The right people on the board will always be harder on themselves than the leader will ever have to be. Your job then is to build your folks up when they feel they are falling down or when they actually do fall.

Aspiring for perfection is fine, not great. However, expecting perfection is always unrealistic. As leaders, why is their frustration directed at employees when they are not perfect? If you know that they will not be perfect, why are you surprised when they are not? Move on and get over it. Your job is to help them be better next time. If you did not help them grow from the mistake, then that is a point where you can get frustrated with yourself. You are missing the chance to truly lead.

The greatest moments of leadership happen when your staff members are in their weakest moments.

LET TRANSPARENCY BE YOUR FRIEND

Seeking clear communication with staff at all times is ideal but difficult to accomplish. When you communicate openly about your decisions and goals, employee performance and challenges, and company operations—modeling transparency to your staff—the greater chance they will provide transparency back to you. Leaders need this feedback because leaders need to know when there is something wrong with staff. Leaders cannot be mind-readers. Having direct transparency with staff creates space within your office where concerns can be discussed. Life and work challenges can then be brought into the office. This new information brought forth from transparency allows you as a leader to understand more about what might be impacting your staff's performance. Creating this culture of transparency with staff builds trust, deepens the bond between members of the organization, and maintains morale in times of stress or discomfort.

Being the beacon of transparency in your office sends the message that this is important to the company and that it is beneficial to everyone involved to be open. When your organization lacks transparency, trust is eroded. After that occurs, words do not matter and good faith follows trust out of the office. Building trust and good faith back into the organization will always be more challenging than being transparent from the beginning. I will repeat...

Building trust and good faith back into the organization will always be more challenging than being transparent from the start.

Once weakened, creating trust and good faith in an organization will always be hard to repair. So, leaders must consider: What are you afraid to be transparent about and how does that compare to the loss of trust and good faith in the office? Additionally, transparency always leads to more respect even if the message is painful. So, be frank and upfront with your staff. They are stronger than you give them credit for.

A final point about transparency. As leaders we should be okay with telling our staff that we cannot be transparent. I have never had a person complain to me when I was transparent about having information that I would not be able to disclose to them. They have always appreciated the honesty about the limitations about what I can or cannot disclose. They are also aware about how their role in the organization influences what information I can or cannot share with them.

Leadership is love happens when leaders model transparency to show to their staff they can also be open. Leaders need to be clear about what they can say and what they cannot. Transparency matters to your staff, and they will appreciate the honesty.

TALK ABOUT PRIORITIES

Talk about priorities early and often. Just as it is extremely important to know your purpose in work, it is just as important to know the priorities of everyone involved with your organization. No one should say in your organization, "Why are we doing this?"

Setting the priorities up front allows staff to know where their needs fall within the organization. As a leader, the goals and objectives from your direct reports and their direct reports should align with the organization's goals and priorities.

However, not every priority should receive equal weight, attention, or importance. Some of the priorities based on the current climate at your organization are valued more than others. Some priorities have time-limited funding. Some priorities are not ongoing. Some priorities just need to be accomplished at certain times of the year. The importance of various priorities differs a lot.

This does not mean that the priorities are not important, but with limited budgets and limited time, certain priorities need to be accomplished first. Thus, priorities need to be set for the organization. Also, if you do not have limited budgets or deadlines, enjoy! You are one of the lucky ones. As a leader, you should expect that your staff will think their objectives, goals, and tasks in work are the highest priority for the organization. They should act that way. After you or your organization sets goals and priorities, as a leader, you let your staff know. I have heard leaders talk about how "everyone needs new shoes." You then need to tell all the staff who are getting "shoes" and who are not. You can then use your priorities to telegraph where the energy, time, or funding is going. When people know the priorities, they can take directions less personally.

At the end of the day, do not lie and tell someone they are the priority and then not treat them like one. People prefer to know where they stand versus being lied to. You as a leader will gain more by being honest with them compared to pandering to their hopes or trying to achieve your hidden motives.

Now that you speak up often about your organization's priorities, you also need to listen to your staff's concerns and worries when they see they are not a higher priority. As a leader, if the person is worried about not being a priority, first listen and then let them know where they fall within the plan.

When working with adults, treat them like adults.

Be transparent about priorities and if you promise a staff member or unit that they are a priority, again—treat them like one. If you learn that the priorities change or you need to change them, follow back up with your folks who thought they were priorities. Once more, be transparent with them. As in the last chapter, being open with staff only helps.

Ultimately, talking about priorities only further helps telegraph your actions. Your staff members can see money being spent, where energy in the organization is being invested, and where leaders are spending their time. When staff see the leaders' language and behaviors align, they know what to expect. When the leaders state they want to give raises and then do not, but staff see the leaders spending money in different areas, staff know what is important to leaders. Now as leaders, we have all spent money on things instead of raises. However, the money spent would not have covered raises, or it was soft money to start. This again is a suitable time for transparency and noting your priorities.

Therefore, be honest about your priorities from the beginning. Talk about them often with your team and note when changes occur with the organization's priorities. Finally, listen to your staff members' concerns when they are not as high on the priority list. Doing these things after you or your organization set the priorities builds trust, respect, and good faith with your staff.

SPEAK DIRECTLY TO THE ISSUE

Early on in my leadership roles, whenever I would run into routine issues that would come up for staff or clients, I would run to my computer and create a new policy to make sure this behavior didn't happen again. I doubt I am the only one who has done this. I suspect individuals reading this might still do this. This is the wrong approach for several reasons, especially when we know leadership is love.

We often change the policy instead of talking directly to the issue. What this means is that leadership will just make new rules, not single out anyone, and then make a new announcement via memo or staff meeting. The absolute worst version of this is the passive aggressive sign. If you want to destroy a work culture, create a sign culture. If you have ever been in a workplace like that, you know what I mean. Unless you are the one who enjoys making the signs.

If that is you, I am glad you are reading this. An easy thing to remember about signs in the office is the following:

If the signs restrict or control, tear them down.

Now the disclaimer, just for the sign-lovers and lawyers. Yes, safety signs, legal signs, and signs about access to spaces need to exist. Those signs in the workplace are important for obvious reasons. Signs about cleaning up, what can be stored in the refrigerator, and messages about microwaving fish do not. I repeat, they do not need to exist in a workplace or anywhere.

Signs are passive. Leaders need to talk directly to the issues. If you cannot speak directly to the issue in the office, then I call that a nonissue. I will explain that in another way.

Leaders focus on things that are important. If the issue is important, signs undermine the importance. If the issue is important and you do not take time to address it, other people in the office will recognize that the issue is not important to you.

Another reason to speak directly to the issue is that sometimes the behaviors you or others are pointing out as problematic in the office are not recognized as being an issue from the person doing it. So, making a general statement will result in the problematic person not even thinking it is about them. Thus, the issues continue in the office and the culture suffers.

Leaders must also embrace their staff's humanity. When we just put up signs we are signaling this is not worth a conversation. Open a dialogue with someone who is engaging in potentially problematic behavior in the office. Open a dialogue that allows us to examine the behavior with curiosity rather than judgment. Leadership will better understand the behavior, and the staff member will gain greater insight into how their behavior is impacting the office.

The other mistake when we do not address the problem is we punish everyone else. How many of us remember as kids when a sibling, teammate, or classmate was acting up and everyone was punished. Those moments were the worst! So, why continue to repeat this pattern? To make things worse, we are not talking about kids anymore. We are talking about adults, fully grown adults! Punishing everyone becomes insulting and is another culture killer. When you treat your best performers the way you treat your lowest performers, expect your best performers to find their way to the door.

Thus, when given the chance to lead, do so by directly addressing the issue. Focus on the issue at hand. Do not engage in sign wars. Address the problem on a case-by-case basis and do not become the place that punishes everyone because of one person's behavior.

DEVELOP A FOXHOLE CULTURE

What is a Foxhole Culture?

I guess you might be thinking, what is a foxhole culture? It was something I found effective in the early 2020s during my time as a leader. Foxhole culture, in a nutshell, is when people have the backs of each other while knowing every contribution is not equal. I realized that, at times, I will give more than others in the workplace. They will seem to have it easy. However, when my moment comes, when I need it easy, others step up for me to relax.

The visual image and experience for this idea comes from soldiers in the military who are in literal foxholes. Both might dig the foxhole, but one is going to get to sleep first. Additionally, if you do not trust the person to stay up while you sleep, you will not be sleeping that long or that well, resulting in a weakened and vulnerable position.

Foxhole culture was developed when people realized things will not always go their way. Regularly, I remind staff about our goal of having a foxhole culture. We discuss how it takes trusting the individual or individuals we are in that foxhole with together. Thus, building this culture requires leaders to work to hire the right people to set up the chessboard, but that alone is not enough to create foxhole culture.

A foxhole culture is cultivated through love.

Without bringing a good-faith approach, trust, and curiosity instead of judgment into the office, as well as modeling a selfless approach as a leader, the foxhole culture is just an idea. Fostering these behaviors and beliefs between staff members enables a foxhole culture. I might even say a foxhole culture in a workplace is actually a reflection of an organization where leadership is love.

The sign you have a foxhole culture is when trust happens and your individual team members accept those moments without gossiping, badmouthing, or having a disgruntled tone. The staff egos are put aside, and leaders do not have a tit-for-tat scorekeeping organization. In a foxhole culture, staff knows when it is time for them to step up for another staff member because others have stepped up for them.

You might ask why a leader would create a foxhole culture. They may believe a foxhole culture will not last and just anger staff. Well, that is an easy answer for me:

It is because life can be a struggle!

We have all had a difficult day or moment at work when someone picked up our slack. We have all had co-workers go through something hard. In all likelihood, when is there NOT someone on your team or within your organization who is facing some challenge in their life or at work?

If life were perfect, planned, and predictable, we would not need leaders because everything would work out. So, when leaders penalize staff members for being human, you are now asking your folks to show up to work with their humanity left at home. That is not leadership as love. In a foxhole culture, leaders embrace the humanity of all staff members, and staff does that with each other. So, let us talk about what holds together and fosters a foxhole culture.

Linchpin of a Foxhole Culture

The linchpin of a foxhole culture is the people and their relationships with each other. It is not fantasy—a foxhole culture is dependent on every staff member pulling their weight. Over time, staff will see who is drawing from the well, but not refilling it. As leaders, you always need to be alert and aware of the status of your organization's foxhole. Foxhole cultures will not flourish if everyone on the team is self-centered or only self-interested. That includes you as the leader.

REMEMBER, THE WORLD IS NOT FAIR

Roles are Different

With clear expectations, make it known that there are different expectations for separate roles. We should always treat individuals equally with respect, care, honesty, and love. Why would we not provide this to our staff? I am writing a book about how leadership is love. However, staff will not be treated equally with work hours, shift report and end times, work tasks, and most importantly, pay. That is not a problem. That is reality. However, it is a problem when you lead everyone to believe that everything in the office is equal at all times, at every minute. As stated earlier, the process of setting expectations and roles, and being transparent, helps create the foxhole culture. Within a foxhole culture, everyone knows the world is not fair.

A culture killer is when individuals think everything is equal. That again exemplifies the importance of being clear. Additionally, from my experience, people that complain the most about fairness likely never see all the work others do in the workplace. Also, those individuals who complain about others frequently do not recognize the luck they possess in their own position. While spending much of the time complaining, self-reflection loses out.

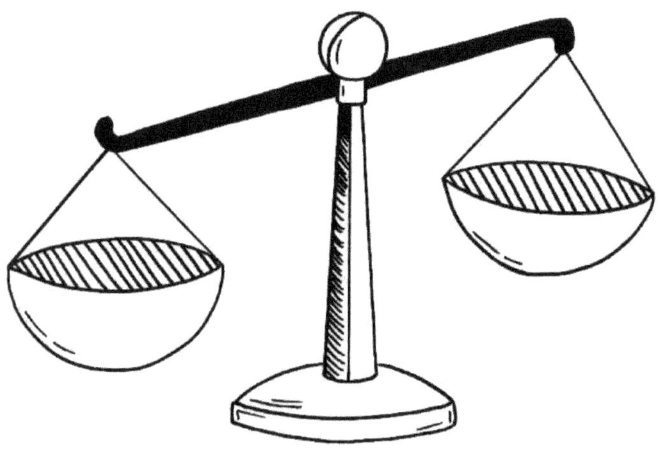

For example, I remember managing complaints about folks who were arriving late to the office and how that is not fair. The people complaining were required to be on time to open, however, they were always wrapped up and out of the office at five p.m. sharp. And I mean sharp! The people they complained about might stroll into work a little late, but they would be lucky to leave at five p.m. Leaving at five p.m. is often a joke for those individuals. The funny thing is the staff members who stayed past five never complained about the individuals leaving at five sharp. Also, the complainers never saw the late work because they were gone. They did not know about it until I told them. A funny thing happened. That group stopped complaining after they realized work looks different for separate groups and roles.

Moreover, nothing pulls at me more than when people complain about leaders not being able to do things employees can do. As leaders, we should be creating teams that bring the best skills together. No one wants to work on a team or for an organization where the leader is the best at everything involving the project or company.

Again, this highlights the importance of expectations and roles. I hope a chief financial officer would be the smartest on financial operations and the information security director would be the best on cybersecurity. I would be disappointed if that organization's leader was the best with both managing financial accounts and cybersecurity. Still, why this pulls at me the most is that I still hear individuals complaining when the roles are clearly different. This is what leads to my frustration. I am frustrated because of the view these individuals have about the role, and I am even more frustrated because no one ever told them about how there are different roles for different positions.

It is also surprising when staff do not see the additional work others in the office do and just assume those other employees are lazy. As leaders, it is vital to make sure all employees know how their role might vary from others in the workplace. Staff need to be reminded that not all work will be witnessed by everyone. Staff should not be keeping tabs on other people's productivity for comparison purposes. After all, leaders need to remember everyone needs respect and everyone needs to remember the world is not fair.

Sometimes We Lose

As this section is titled, this is true for all leaders. If a leader tells you that they never have lost in their life, then they have never truly led. Leaders have always lost at some point in their lives and careers. I could draft a whole book on all my losses, but that is for another day. However, these losses help make leaders better. Losses allow leaders to stay attuned and be aware that there is a loss always around the corner.

The way we get through losses in our life as leaders is by having support. It is the people next to us who will help us get back up. There will be times when you will have to be helped up and times when you will help others up. This is the beauty of leadership being love. In the face of defeat, relationships and love will help us all through that dark moment. Even after some of the worst defeats, leaders need to do three things with their supports: persist, regroup, and re-engage.

Persist: Keep moving forward and do not quit. You may be asked to slow down if needed, but without stopping.

Regroup: Evaluate future plans and goals. Then build mental strength, relationships, and knowledge that align with your goals.

Re-engage: Move toward the future again. Lean into the hard work and challenges required to meet your goals.

Leaders who persist, regroup, and re-engage realize the world is not fair and still face it.

...WORK TO MAKE IT FAIR

Equity not Equality

When we do work, I believe in equity. For me this means we must recognize hard work differently from routine work. I believe one of the worst things we can do is recognize folks that go the extra mile the same way we recognize folks that just punch in and out on their timecard. This is not fair to your staff. I believe in paying folks fairly. Trust me, the hardest workers know how hard everyone else works. Do not slap your hardest workers in the face. They are the ones you want to retain and keep in your culture.

Paying your best workers the same as your less productive workers is unfair to the hardest workers. If you pay equally across the board, be ready for the best to leave and the worst to stay.

For example, at a previous workplace, my wife became frustrated on my behalf when she noticed that folks who did not work as hard as me got paid the same as me. I always told her, "They are the smart ones—getting paid the same and doing less." I was willing to continue for a while and the situation resolved itself in the end. Feeling the way I did, and knowing how others may feel, leads me to not want others to experience this as well. Leaders work to make the world fair. We can all do a better job. Pay a living wage no matter their background and position. Pay more for experience, expertise, and effort, which are never equal. That is what is fair. This is leadership as love. Now, I know what you are thinking, *Man, this guy has a huge blind spot.* I would like to believe it is not huge and we all have blind spots. That is why when thinking about pay, remember two things. Money matters, as you remember from the earlier chapters. Never make personnel and salary decisions without talking with your mentor or vault. You will learn about vaults soon. They will help make sure you are not bringing biases to the hiring and negotiation tables.

Interns and Senior Staff

Another problematic situation is when interns and senior staff have the same rules and procedures. This issue is one that really annoys me. It should be a simple thing—leaders ought to be able to make different rules within the workplace. In my workplace, we recognize that individuals with independent licenses can make choices regarding the treatment of our clients as they see fit once the therapy office door is closed. It is not fair to treat independently licensed providers like unlicensed staff.

Do aspects of your organization do the same?

When leaders treat staff with expertise like mechanized cogs, continue to watch that expertise walk out the door. Do not be that leader. This never ends well for your organization.

When we do not treat expertise like what it is worth, hiding behind the view that it is about fairness, they will go where they will be treated equal to their worth. Individuals will go where they believe they will be treated and compensated per their internal value. Leadership must meet staff where they are and be fair about it. Treating all your staff at the level of the lowest trained and least experienced member just holds everyone back. Leaders must believe more in their senior staff's ability to make the right decisions to allow them to dream big and achieve greater things in their career.

The world is not fair, but work to make it fair one hire at a time, one decision at a time, and with all your relationships. Yes, all your relationships matter, treat them the way they need to be treated. That is fair.

LEAN INTO YOUR POWER

I always get disappointed when people talk about "eliminating their power" or "removing their power" in relationships as well as within their work. There are two things that really bug me about that statement. First, can you really eliminate your power or are you just pretending it is gone? Second, sometimes power can be leveraged to make things better. I like to think about it as...

Leveraging power for good.

So, what do I do when those are my big concerns? I do two things: I always acknowledge my power and do not act like it does not exist in spaces where it does. I learned to lean into my power.

I am not afraid to put my power on the table and move from there in my relationships and leadership rather than trying to hide it. Acknowledging power allows me to work with it. It often seems in my line of work that power is a four-letter word. With that in mind, I want to talk more about how power can be helpful in the workplace, unavoidable, and in the end, be a good thing.

Power with Your Staff

When we hide our power to try and make people feel like it does not exist, we are tricking folks into a false sense of security. I would rather be transparent and acknowledge my power. I believe this is what creates a true level of security in those dynamics.

For example, I have been supervising trainees for more than ten years now. As I have spent more time supervising, my power throughout the years has also increased. The trainees are in the same position throughout the years, but my role continues to advance. What I learned from these experiences is how trainees treat you differently when your power increases.

So, what I learned over the years is you cannot pretend about power. As my power increased, I talked about it more and more in supervision. The funny thing is, my relationships with trainees through the years continue to be deep and meaningful even in the face of increased power. Thus, power in your relationship with staff should not be avoided; you just need to own it.

Power within Your Organization

As stated earlier, leaning into power can make changes that we did not think were ever possible before. This part is really meant for the young leaders reading this book. Way too often young leaders are afraid of their power. They have learned that power is bad. Bad people have power. Power corrupts individuals. The list could go on. Now, while this is all possible, I ask young leaders to reflect on themselves regarding these concerns. What do they know about their values, principles, and morals? They better not forget them. Leaders should also find people they can go to who can be honest with them. That is your "vault." You will learn about this in the next chapter. A vault is extremely important when learning to manage your power for good.

Leaders who leverage their power for good can change organization structures and morale for the better. I remember early on in my leadership a staff member asked if they could go home early. At that point, I realized I really control when people can come or go in the office. The power of being able to send someone home early or have them come in late can be leveraged when staff have hard days with crisis appointments or struggles at home. The power we have can change a staff member's day for the better. This is using power for good.

When leaders are in control of organizational structures and vacancies occur, leaders can reassess and change the structure to make a better place for staff to work.

Use your power to make the organization better.

Too often, leaders see the structure they are in at the company and accept it. I want you to challenge that belief in yourself and within the organization. Use your power to make the change that best supports your organization, product, and customers. Most importantly, as I say throughout this book, use the power to support your staff. I like to remind leaders, if you control change in your organization, you can make things better for all within your organization.

A final note about having power in structures or organizations. If you have power and complain about nothing changing, look to whom you are complaining. With your power, find other people in power and speak with them. Too many folks with power complain to individuals who have the same power or no power. The funny thing is those folks also complain that nothing changes. So, with your power, lean into it, and find spaces where power exists where you can lead and advocate for changes. You do not have to accept the status quo. Work to make a difference around you. To me, that is the best use of power!

Power, as you can see, cannot be avoided in leadership. A leader's power must be embraced. Once you accept that truth, you can move forward as a leader to use it for good in your organization. When you do use it for good, do so to help those who do not have the power yet and those who will never have the power.

FIND YOUR "VAULT"

There was a *Seinfeld* episode I watched in college. The show was worth having the box set, so I watched a lot of *Seinfeld.* You can learn a lot of what not to do from *Seinfeld.* However, this particular episode made a difference for me. There was a scene between the characters where they discussed "vaulting" information they did not want others to know. Meaning what someone tells you or you tell someone will never, I mean never, be disclosed to other people. Ever since this episode, I learned how powerful it is to have yourself a vault. Just make sure to find a true vault, not someone like Jerry who does not actually keep the information vaulted.

The vault you have is important for talking over your fears, frustrations, risks, and ridiculous ideas or aspirations.

Vault relationships are special. Often, they are one of a kind. They are some of the deepest and most vulnerable relationships you will find in the workplace or life. Having a vault is different from a mentor, different from a boss, and different from a spouse. However, a vault could be one of those individuals. A vault is truly someone equal to you in that conversation. Rank and relationship do not matter. What matters in that moment is that your vault and you are unfiltered and raw. In that moment, expect to be vulnerable because there is no need for impression management and no feelings to protect between each other. These are the moments of realism, the moments that are rarely seen in professional settings, especially where your direct reports are present.

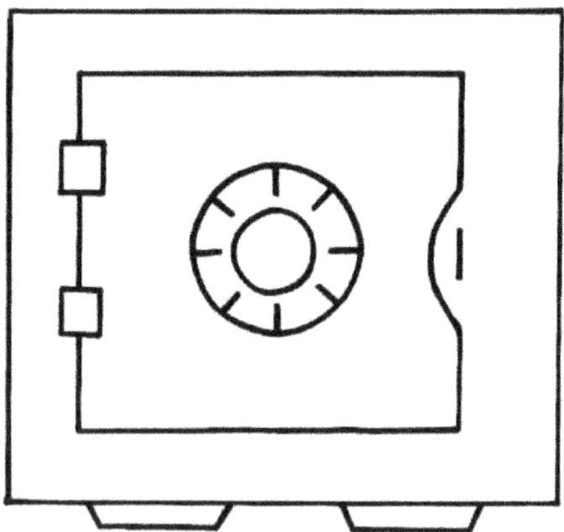

You might be reading and thinking these conversations are where terrible things or dreadful things happen. Everyone should challenge this thought. I believe it is because of these conversations that terrible things do *not* happen. These interactions are where you should be called out on your stupid, self-centered, short-sighted, boneheaded, and/or stubborn ideas. This is actually why vaults are good to have in a leader's life. Talking with your vault allows for free thinking while not being judged or having your value held to a thought. It allows for frustrations that never turn into anything more than venting or blowing off steam. The vault allows for thoughts to be just that—thoughts.

Having a vault in your life will make your work better because they will not treat you like a boss. They will treat you like a creative, bold, visionary, flawed leader, but most importantly they will treat you like YOU. The you that brings your whole self to work every day. You, the individual who is just being human at work.

MAKE WINS FOR EVERYONE A GOAL

When leading I have found that you cannot always make everyone happy. I found that out the hard way, with a lot of stress, and now less hair. I learned that people will hold grudges. They will hold grudges when you were clear ahead of time with plans or decisions and even when you do so without ill intent. Still, fear of grudges and dislike should never stop you from trying to help everyone win.

You can't make everyone happy, but you can help everyone win.

As a leader, you might not be recognized for your wins. In the end, your goal should be to get everyone to win. If the goal you set is accomplished, no matter who is recognized, you have a win. Who cares if you do not get the credit. Just make sure your staff members are recognized for their wins.

The goal of leading is not self-interest when you practice leadership as love. It is always about building up the team or the organization. As a leader, spread out wins as much as you can.

Remember, in the end, creating wins for others will always create wins for you. This holds true from frontline workers, to the top of the organization, to any local or global partnerships. There really are no exceptions to this concept when you are a leader within your organization. Now outside of the organization, I am extremely competitive. I still believe, however, there are ways to lift all ships for a better world when partnerships occur that benefit all involved. Find those opportunities and leaders will find wins.

I think often about my grandfather, or as I called him *Gido,* saying that he wishes well on others as well as on himself. His life was not a zero-sum life. He was highly successful, but not at the expense of others around him. We as leaders should always be looking for ways to bring others in and up. Build relationships with others that advance everyone's needs. This does not mean that everyone knows why it is good to partner, but as a leader your goal is to help others see the possibilities together. Leaders share these visions with others. But such visions can only be shared through relationships. So, what can you do?

Make them!

Build Coalitions, Not Islands

Building coalitions and not islands is good policy both internally within the organization and outside the organization. The best way to build coalitions is when leaders can find individuals with similar purposes and goals. Magic happens when individuals who share purposes and goals work together within and outside your workplace. Once you have your chessboard set up with the right people and vision, individuals will want to join up and work together.

When you lead on an island, you lose resources, ideas, and growth. With coalitions you can leverage the resources together and do things bigger than you and your organization have ever done before. Often, what is done together is greater than what individuals can do separately. Additionally, the ideas that come from the coalitions between organizations will move you and your company forward. Once you build coalitions, everyone in this coalition wins and the people you serve or products you make win too! Again, make wins for everyone and people will be happy.

Create Allies Not Enemies

You create allies when you help possible partners or staff see the actions you are taking, or requesting them to take, are mutually beneficial to all parties involved. When they see the results of your actions, those individuals will become supporters of your organization's mission. When allies outside of my department realize they will benefit from my goals, those departments openly support us. When I see their department goals benefit my area, we actively support them, and everyone wins.

So, what happens when you work to make everyone win within your department or company?

Everyone wins!

Yup! Leaders should be working within their specific units or organizations to help everyone win. When you can do this, you can start chipping away at egos within the organization. This shows that leaders hold no secret motives and helps your employees to build trust with leadership. Once employees see what leaders are doing is helpful to them, their defenses will drop.

Be an asset to others, not an adversary.

So, now that we know that making wins for everyone is good for everyone involved, leaders need to focus on making wins for everyone by building coalitions and having allies. How then do you build coalitions and allies as leaders? Leaders do this through relationships. These relationships are built because of leaders who understand leadership is love.

Finally, leaders must persist and not let their ego get in the way of creating wins. If what you want accomplished occurs and you do not get credit or recognized, remember your goal was still successful. Give credit like you give love: selflessly, freely, unconditional, and plenty. Believe me. When you give out credit, it shall return.

EMPOWER AND EXPECT AN EMPOWERED RESPONSE

I find it funny when leaders talk about empowering their employees and then say they are disappointed when the staff act empowered. One of my goals as a leader is for staff to feel empowered. I want them to talk back, ask challenging questions, and be advocates for themselves. Why then would I feel surprised or offended when they act empowered?

Because I am a little rebellious, my leadership style creates a culture that allows for empowerment in the office. What culture do you bring into the office? Do you bring an empowered mentality, rule follower, punish back-stab/gossip, fun/joyful, or rebellious culture? I know there is more a leader can bring into the office. However, I think those are good starting points to reflect on as leaders. I know which one or ones I would like to bring into the office. I hope you have an insight into what you bring to the workplace.

Do you know what you bring and what you want to create?

Now, being empowered does not excuse problematic or rude behavior. Tact and professionalism should be expected in the workplace. So, what is an example of an empowered response that is not rude or lacking tact? Take a look at this one:

Leader: Can you take this appointment for me?

Staff: Sorry, I can't. I am feeling a little backed up with my paperwork.

So, what is there to be disappointed about in this situation?

There is one thing to be disappointed about, and it is not the staff member's response. My disappointment rests with the leader. Did you guess it right? Let me review this example.

When you empower your staff and enter with that question, nothing good comes to the leader. If taking the appointment was an option, the appointment still remains on the leader. If the situation was not an option and you did not give it to the staff member, then you are overloaded. If not taking the appointment was never an option and now you made the staff member take the appointment, you have now disempowered them. The last one I consider to be the worst option.

For folks who think in this example that it's the staff member who is not a team player, you are wrong.

The leader gave the option. Leaders should not be acting or talking with hidden messages. We should be clear and transparent about the meaning of the interaction. Additionally, when we empower our staff, they become advocates for themselves. In this example, the staff member knows they are backed up a bit. A healthy culture would lead us to believe the staff member was being honest and not just avoiding work. Thus, as leaders, we must empower our staff and know when they do not have an option. Do not give them a false sense of empowerment.

So, let us try this again. It might look funny and not feel empowered, but this is a moment when the option to refuse is not there. Still, the leader uses open communication, not offering an option when there is none:

Leader: I have an appointment I need you to take.

Staff: Okay.

Leader: Do you have any questions? And how can I support you with this change?

In an empowered culture, the staff knows when there is an option to say no and when there is not. One way they know is because the leader is clear about when situations are optional. Leaders in empowered cultures also support staff members through challenges when things are out of the staff member's control. Empowered cultures bring the best traits out of a staff member. Leading is not about creating hidden tests or fear of noncompliance within the workplace. Leadership is love when we empower staff and therefore create an empowered organization.

KNOW WHY THE POLICY EXISTS

Policies Aren't Sacred

I love to say, "I am married only to my wife." Meaning, of course, that I'm not married to policies.

I regularly say this to others regarding questions or ideas to change something within our department policies or operations. It might feel strange to you about why I mention this in this chapter, but for me the reason is clear. As leaders, if we do not know why the policy exists and/or the purpose of the policy, then we should be open to changing the policy. When we do not know why a policy exists, we set ourselves up for trouble down the road. This lack of knowledge not only affects our strategies and efficiencies, but it negatively impacts staff and their feelings toward the workplace. Take for instance these statements:

- It's just the way it is.

- It has always been this way.

- I don't know why we do that.

If these statements are something you have heard before, I bet they made you cringe as they do to me. If you have said that before and have neither figured out how nor tried to improve the situation, sadly, I cringe again. We should always be looking for ways to improve the operations of the office. When we get complacent with operations, this chapter writes itself. But beyond the bottom line, we lose credibility with staff and that is then transferred to the customer.

Take this personal experience I had when I attempted to pay my student loans. (Yes, I had student loans. When I meet millennials without student loans, I am always impressed!) So, I was on the phone with the student-loan lender, wanting to get a payment error fixed. The customer service representative was not helping me or clarifying the reason behind the issue. So, I asked to speak to the manager. Yes, it really got to that point for me because I hate pulling that let-me-talk-to-your-manager card. I then was told that I could not speak to the manager, and they would call me if I requested it. I asked if this is policy, and the representative indicated it was policy. I asked her why this was policy, and her response was "I don't know, but it is policy." Talk about killing any relationship or credibility that worker might have had with me. So, to end this story, the representative indicated the manager would follow up with me 36-48 hours later. If they did not call me back, I was to call again to request they call me again. So, their policy after they screwed up was for me to call back if they screwed up by not calling me. To this day, I still have never been called. My student loans are paid off now, though.

Rebellious Reasons

I am a little rebellious, and someone who does not like rules. Yes, I know, super edgy, right? But seriously, I am not a huge fan of rules. I really dislike rules that are not clear about why they exist. So, rules and policies really need to be vital to operations to exist in my office. Other leaders who can relate to me on these past couple statements must also realize this is not an excuse to be unethical. For leaders who are lovers of rules, lighten up!

Organizational policies should allow for flexibility. Your general counsel might not like this, but they should. Sometimes breaking the rules is bad and we should hold folks accountable. Sometimes not following the rules is the right thing to do. This is because following the rules often upholds the status quo. If you like the status quo, you probably would not be reading this book right now. So, this is why going against the rules sometimes is what is needed to make the organization better. Sometimes the world requires leaders to be radical—acting against the status-quo.

Still, what makes the leader truly more of a "rebel" is if they take their policies, rules, or any other manual, and remove anything that is not essential to the safety of their staff and individuals in their organization. I would say that is pretty "bad ass" if you were to do this as a leader. I will tell you from my experience, we continue to work within my department to make our operations manual no more than safety and how things work within our office for our clinical staff who are independently licensed. Interns will always have more rules. Again, the goal is not to over-restrict our staff. Therefore, when leaders review company policies, make sure you and your staff know why the policies matter. If you cannot tell staff why it truly matters, get rid of the policy.

LEARN WHO IS HUNGRY

Young bloods and the inexperienced are often "hungry" to achieve. Yet lately, I hear employers talk and complain about the "new generation" as being lazy and not interested in working. Often saying, "When I was their age…"

I bet you could fill in a lot from just your own conversations with employers. Today it seems perfectly acceptable to engage in this kind of talk about our youth. Even my own father, whom I deeply respect, speaks a lot of the younger generation being lazier than prior generations. I often respond by highlighting how his generation was likely perceived as lazy because they only had to work five-day work weeks. The response makes him pause and reflect. I always appreciate his honest takes and opinions, as well as how new information makes him pause and rethink his position.

Additionally, the "panic" over younger generations being lazy and disrespectful has been seen since ancient Greece. So, I deeply believe every generation has hungry individuals. You just need to get them on the chessboard. Moreover, you will find success when you allow them to be hungry at work and let them achieve.

Here is why you as a leader need to step back and let this younger crop of workers be hungry. They want to make change. They have fresh ideas. Their energy level is high, and they are ready to launch. A leader's job is to allow them to fly. But remember, you will regularly act as ground control. You are the one setting the guardrails. Final decisions will frequently come from you. This is because leaders often have a more panoramic view, but when you see this young group fly, the view can be astonishing.

Making Change

What I find with every new batch of employees is that they

look to do something different than the folks before them. From my start, I always looked to be a change agent and thought that was special. However, like I said, every new batch will have some change agents. When you find them, hold on, because they will let you know the future and see the currents. As a leader, can you allow them to take you there? If you can, they can keep you and your organization fresh.

Fresh Ideas

So, what comes with these change agents are fresh ideas. Some ideas put forth have been done before and that is where a leader's wisdom comes in. In your workplace, your job is to listen to all the ideas, good or bad and old or new. Stay curious with your younger staff. There is a lot they bring into the office. Listening to those fresh ideas will help you and others see so many ways you and your organization can move forward into the future or simply be better. Remember this requires you not only to listen to the ideas, but to seek out those ideas.

High Energy

Once you seek and listen to the change agents, buckle up. They will come at you fast and ready to launch. The good news is you should have some wisdom on the best ways to execute these fresh ideas. What I find most exciting is these individuals will have the energy to see these changes through. This energy is the most important aspect of finding the truly hungry individuals in the office. They see things through. Lean into those strengths they bring and allow them to flow like the current.

One final note on finding workers who are hungry: Leaders need to feed them. Now, I love a meal, and a work-catered meal is even better. What I am talking about, though, is opportunity. When you hold staff back, they will get bored and stale. Think of a campfire—feed it to keep it burning hot and feed it at a steady pace. Help them achieve their dreams. Do not overwhelm your staff or put out their fire. Leaders might make mistakes in timing and workloads in the beginning. That is okay. Through stronger relationships and leading with love, leaders will learn each employee's pace.

SEEK WISDOM AND OPINIONS

Just because you have aged or worked does not mean you have wisdom; wisdom is earned by age and experience. Seeking wisdom always gives insight to leaders who are on any journey in life. The individual you can start to seek wisdom from is anyone who has lived more than you have and/or lived a different life. What is beautiful about this perspective is it does not matter their title, position, or profession. When we are curious and open to others, we learn about ourselves, others, and opportunities.

Wisdom is likely always around you.

As a leader, you might miss out on insights when you look for wisdom based only on visual success, professions, or positions. The best way to find wisdom is to look for someone older than yourself and then listen. You will learn pretty quickly that they have insight on life, themselves, and others. When you discover that they do, you will find a person who can reflect, and through their reflection you will see a lot about this world.

In your organization, seek views and listen for wisdom. Always make sure to inform the frontline, from lower-level staff to C-suite peers, that their opinion is valid and highly requested because it makes all work better in your organization. With strong relationships in the workplace, the staff will provide you with more opinions. When leadership is love, they will be more willing to open up to you. Your next task as a leader will be wading through which opinions and wisdom you will apply to your organization or yourself.

Avoid Feedback Frustration

There is always one caveat to seeking wisdom and opinions. All workers and mentors need to be aware that opinions and insights will forever be requested, but that does not guarantee that opinions will get implemented. Sometimes that is a hard pill for a staff member to swallow. Nonetheless, it is always better to be clear and transparent than to lead them on with unrealistic expectations.

Way too often, staff become discouraged when their opinions are not implemented. What I hear from those individuals is, "Why would you want to know what I think if you never do it." Opinions are wonderful; I view seeking opinions like brainstorming. When you frame it this way, staff understand from the beginning that the questions asked are about seeking thoughts.

So, be clear in the beginning that not all opinions will come to reality. That still does not decrease the value of opinions. Leaders must start this at onboarding or the beginning of a conversation. It is important to set that understanding from the start. Doing so will decrease pressure to be perfect as well as discomfort among employees. Thoughts, opinions, and wisdom are wonderful to have in the workplace. Work as a leader to make sure employees continue to share their opinions. You can often tell the strength of an organization, not from the content of the opinion or thought, but that the staff are willing to share them.

When staff do give you suggestions or opinions, do not just say thank you and walk away. If you do that, they will feel disrespected, deflated, and devalued. Take the time to discuss their ideas with them. Explore pros and cons together. They may realize on their own that their ideas are not so great, and you will not have to tell them why. If their suggestions have merit, talk about the options for implementation. Recognize your staff members' humanity by giving a thoughtful response to suggestions important to your staff.

Don't lose your humanity by failing to see

the humanity in others.

PART IV

The Cosmos Connects

Close your eyes and start looking.

THE PARADOX

Part IV is entitled "The Cosmos Connects" because everything I have written in this book is interconnected. It always has been connected. This interconnectedness exists for no known reason, and this is okay. The why has always been a beautiful mystery. Like a stream that constantly flows, its water is connected to the land. While the stream is forever changing, neither that land nor the water have complete control over the path of the current.

This is the paradox of this book. I present all these things to do and at the same time I accept how we control so little. Once this interconnectedness of your world is understood, seen, and accepted, there is peace in understanding that leaders cannot control everything. Although, through connection all can and will change. Leaders will grow when they acknowledge this belief in their life. It is powerful when you as a leader allow the iron fist of control to loosen and let life flow forward.

Let your hand hold to comfort rather than to hold back.

LEADERSHIP HAS ALWAYS BEEN BIGGER THAN YOU

Please do not think you are the only reason things are working well in your organization. Remember what I said about luck: It could be the right place, right time, and so many other reasons why things are working well. Avoid the pitfall of your ego. Hubris can be a leader's arch enemy.

You are always a part of something bigger when things are going well.

Do not forget that. Enjoy the success of the community you are a part of. When there is joy, always welcome it and pass it on. Success of an organization is dependent on many small pieces working together. As Aristotle argued, "the whole is greater than the sum of its parts." The success of your organization is always greater than the sum of the small wins. It is not about great individuals; it is about the great team that made it work. Therefore, I always encourage individuals to be a part of something bigger than themselves. It is healthy to remember we are not the center of the world.

The greatest aspect of being a part of something bigger than yourself is that it reminds us that we are in this together. It demonstrates the importance of community in our lives. As a leader who has led, followed, listened, spoken, watched, and acted, I can attest that being part of a community helps everyone grow. I sure have experienced this growth personally and have also observed this growth in others I have worked with. When leaders build communities, they not only build coalitions, they build strong individuals. The community created expands when those individuals move on, move up, or settle in. Seeing those communities, people, and relationships expand is one of the most exciting things about building relationships. As a leader, you are in the driver's seat in creating community.

Change Through Relationships

I am a leader and someone who advocates for the importance of relationships in our lives. Relationships of love improve each other's lives. This includes relationships at work. We as leaders should recognize that working together to improve each other's lives is the same goal in the workplace.

Work within an organization does not excel until the relationships within the workplace flourish.

Everything you have read in this book is about relationships. Relationships do not start without your help. However, relationships are dependent on more than one person. Relationships are everything in the workplace and it will take time to build those relationships between all workers. Be patient and steady with your staff. Change within your organization is going to be waiting on the success of relationships you and your team create within your workplace.

Leaders can establish the course and set up culture, but your staff are the ones who really make the culture.

Leaders can create signals for work culture, yet staff are the ones who act out the aspirations of the organization. They are the ones who get your organization to the horizon and beyond. Make an environment that makes your staff want to engage, create joy, and provide opportunities. Help staff see the possibilities. Collaborate with them to see that possibilities are always greater with more parties involved. Help your staff want to drink to a toast!

Leadership is, and the organization is, always bigger than you as the leader. Never forget that, but also never forget that change within an organization can start with you. Finally, remember the following:

Leaders work to foster relationships within their organizations. Through those relationships, communities are built. Culture then flows from those communities.

INSPIRATIONS

The focus of this entire book is how leadership is love, and that as a leader, I am living this experience.

The individuals who influenced the ideas that make leadership as love a possibility also inspired this book. Some of these inspirations are people I currently work with or have worked with in the past. Some of the influences are family. However, all these inspirations are individuals who personally influenced me to think this way about leadership. And that is the beauty of inspiration—it can come from anywhere. These individuals are older, younger, related, not related, a superior, a subordinate, or peer. Again, anyone in your life can be inspiring. Leaders just need to look.

Accordingly, what you see in each of the profiles of inspirational individuals highlighted earlier in the book is the underlying care they have for others in their world. These individuals not only care for others, but they also live the ideas in this book. They might not realize it because it comes so easy to them, but these individuals are profoundly unique in these behaviors. In my life I have interacted with thousands of people. These people are different.

Find the different people in your life and be inspired.

You may ask when reflecting on the inspirations I provided: *Why are there not more single stories that highlight such great qualities?* Well, for me it was not ever about single events; single events are powerful, but these individuals are more about their whole way of being. That is what is so powerful about the people I have discussed and why they inspire me. It was not a simple act, but a way of being with others. When the essence of the individual is inspirational it is easy to believe the world is changing for the better. So, I appeal to you as a leader to inspire others.

Be in the chapter of someone's book!

As a leader, and more importantly, as a human, we have the chance every day to make an impact on someone's life. Be that person in someone else's life. A beautiful thing about recognizing how leadership is love is you might already be inspiring someone and not even know it. These individual's actions are the true examples of how little choices can have enormous impact on other people's lives. There are not enough pages in this book to express my gratitude to these individuals and all the other countless individuals who have inspired me in my life. These people inspire, no matter their career, generation, or life experience. This is what truly makes so many people in my life special.

So, the couple of inspirations I chose to highlight are in my life—I know if you look around in your own life, you will find inspiring people as well. If you do not believe me, I have some advice. First, you must have your eyes open and then keep looking. My eyes were open for the individuals I highlight in the book, but they had to be to see the gift. This is why I implore you to look. Second, soak the lessons in. Live the inspiration and share what you have learned from them. Finally, give more. The more you give, the more the world becomes inspired. I am grateful that I was able to highlight the ones in my life. Find the inspirations in your life and be grateful too!

CLOSING TIME

If you are a leader, you know leading is not easy. It never was. Humans are messy and need a lot of care. Work is hardly neat. Challenges will always present themselves in the workplace. Trying to control the mess with rules and rigidity does not make it any easier. As I have said before, having rigid rules actually makes the work harder for everyone involved. Too many rules lead to many more mistakes for staff. Too many rules in the workplace will always lead to more oversight. Leaders or their staff then take much more time and responsibility to make sure all those rules are followed. This keeps organizations from doing the work they originally existed to do. It takes leaders away from building relationships in the workplace. Leadership is love when we move away from control, fear, indifference, and rigidity. Leadership is about allowing others to grow.

We also lose humanity in our workplace when our employees leave their humanity at the door. We cannot be afraid or fear our staff's humanity. When leadership is love, we allow staff to come to work as their whole selves. Leadership as love allows you to bring your whole self too. Allowing staff and yourself to be whole in the workplace has so much to do with trust and vulnerability.

Are you ready to do this?

I hope you are. To get this far in the book and not be willing to try this out would be disappointing. I would suspect fear causes the hesitation. I recognize that leading is not easy. Moreover, I draw a hard line when we refuse to act because of fear. We are being selfish when we let fear control our decisions. Leaders who do not want the experience of discomfort do not really want to lead. I might even go as far to say they are not ready to lead.

Fear and discomfort, though, are really just part of being human. So, I ask myself to withhold judgment and wonder more about the reasoning behind the fear and discomfort in so many leaders. My question for you when you hold the fear and discomfort is simple: Are you ready to ask yourself the hard questions about how and why fear and discomfort present themselves in your workplace? Trepidation in leadership is natural. It really will never go away as long as we continue to grow in the organization. So, focus on the relationships with staff and all the good and bad that come from allowing them to bring their humanity to work. Practice leadership as love through relationships. Relationships will quiet the sounds of fear and discomfort.

Step away from fear and control and discover that leadership is love.

Take the suggestions in this book and see the impact leadership is love will have on your workplace and yourself. The outcomes for your organization will be great. The effect on your team will be even greater. What I have found from living this kind of leadership is a sense of pride in seeing staff succeed. When you practice leadership as love, other leaders will see the benefits too.

In my work, I saw staff believe in themselves more, take bolder risks, ask harder questions, cry a lot, and laugh even more. Their belief in themselves showed in their work with clients, in the wonderful outcomes with clients, the center's morale, and in all their professional success. Standing out the most to me is how everyone in the office grew personally as individuals and together as a team. This is how leadership is love. The staff cares deeply for each other in the same way

I care for them. They want each other to bring their humanity into the office as well. They now understand how leadership is love and they are living it too. Through our relationships, staff members flourish in the workplace.

So, enjoy the challenges, share the purpose, focus on relationships and remember leadership is love.

Now, back to the beginning of the book. These three individuals show up to a bar. They are an optimist, an idealist, and a realist. They sit down with each other and have a couple of drinks together. The optimist sees a workplace that can improve and be better than it currently is functioning. The idealist believes there are ways workplaces can change. The realist states this is how we can do it. This is what the book lays out. It was a lofty goal, but I hope you are able to see it too. Leadership is love because of all these beliefs.

Cheers!

If not for today,

then for tomorrow.

RADICAL/PRACTICAL NOTES

QUICK TAKEAWAYS

The Radical Idea

➤ Leadership Is Love

Leadership is love (LIL) when we see the whole person in the office. LIL is about creating true relationships with staff because the relationship is the heart of any organization. It is knowing how others want to be led and leading the way you would want to be led. LIL is not being selfish and giving feedback as well as giving love. LIL is listening to stories and telling them, being mentored, and mentoring. LIL is also thinking with curiosity, acting with gratitude, embracing our humanity, and dreaming bigger for others.

➤ Think with Curiosity

Thinking with curiosity (TWC) is not rushing to judgment, acting in good faith, and not jumping to conclusions. TWC is being open to continuous learning and a willingness to grow from others.

➤ Act with Gratitude

Acting with gratitude is saying thank you, valuing anyone no matter their title, and understanding the gift of time. Appreciating staff lets you be a part of their journey.

➤ Embrace Our Humanity

Embracing our humanity (EOH) is realizing you and others make mistakes. EOH is owning our mistakes with others and being willing to learn from said mistakes. EOH is having enough character to say sorry and mean it. It is the ability to not be stubborn and not set in one's ways. EOH is being in touch with one's emotions but not letting them dictate an experience or overpower staff feelings.

➤ Dream Bigger for Others

Dreaming bigger for others (DBFO) is believing in staff more than they believe in themselves. DBFO is realizing the potential people have and helping them achieve that potential. DBFO is knowing there is more an individual can attain than what they present on day one.

➤ It's the Relationship, Stupid

Leadership and culture are rooted in relationships. Without relationships, the organization fails. LIL is channeled through the relationship between staff and their leadership. It is allowing the staff to present at work with their humanity and, as leaders, help them accomplish their goals.

The Practical

➤ Recognize the Luck

Leaders work hard and must also realize the breaks that went their way along their career.

➤ Realize What Matters to Them Matters to You

Leaders take interest in their staff's lives and care about what is meaningful to them.

➤ Enjoy Challenges

Leaders face challenges every day. Learn to enjoy challenges because challenges are the job.

➤ Use a Data-Informed Mindset

Staff cannot be reduced to data points. Data alone never tells the whole story. Take in all the information including wisdom and experiences to make decisions.

➤ Signal Your Team

Short meaningful messages create connectedness to your office's purpose.

➤ Set up Your Chessboard

Get the right people on your team in the right places and watch them excel in their roles.

➤ Choose People over Work

Work will always be there; your staff might not be. Take time for them when they need it.

➤ Create an Experience

Experiences will keep your staff around when all other factors are equal, so make them impactful.

➢ Allow People to Let You Down

Trust only occurs when there is a possibility that someone might not succeed or follow through. Growth only happens when mistakes are possible.

➢ Let Transparency Be Your Friend

Leaders should not add more secrecy than warranted. Be transparent with staff.

➢ Talk about Priorities

Leaders talk about priorities and when they change. Be honest with staff about what matters.

➢ Speak Directly to the Issue

Leaders talk directly with/to the concerns. Leaders do not change a system-wide policy because of one bad apple or one mistake.

➢ Develop a Foxhole Culture

Foxhole culture is being able to trust someone to have your back, and they trust you will have their back when they need it from you.

➤ Remember the World Is Not Fair…

Leaders recognize the world is not fair and do not shy away from talking about how we have different rules and responsibilities.

➤ …Work to Make It Fair

Leaders work to make the workplace a better place for all. Leaders recognize that fair does not always mean equal, but equity.

➤ Lean into Your Power

Leaders have power and leaders use the power for good.

➤ Find Your "Vault"

Leaders need to have a person whom they can confide in about difficult topics.

➤ Make Wins for Everyone a Goal

The goal is not to make everyone happy, but if a leader can get a win for everyone, why not try?

➢ **Empower and Expect an Empowered Response**

Leaders who empower staff must expect an empowered response; therefore leaders need to be clear with individuals about asks, needs, and musts.

➢ **Know Why the Policy Exists**

Leaders know why every policy was written, and if they do not know, then leaders work to get rid of it.

➢ **Learn Who Is Hungry**

Motivated staff are the future of the organization. Leaders need to feed them opportunities.

➢ **Seek Wisdom and Opinions**

Leaders seek wisdom from anyone who is willing to share. Leaders must get feedback from stakeholders.

The Cosmos Connects

➤ The Paradox

Leadership is Love is about learning practical ways to lead an office. At the same time, LIL recognizes that control of the office culture has always been in the hands of the staff.

➤ Leadership Has Always Been Bigger than You

Culture is created by the people. Leaders just influence the culture. Create an environment for love and watch it spread.

➤ Inspirations

Open your eyes. Inspirations are always around leaders.

Acknowledgements

I would like to thank my family for their unwavering support. I express my gratitude to my two sons, Harrison and Grant, for their distractions and interest in my work. Both are greatly welcomed. I am grateful for my wife Melissa and her assistance and support in the writing of this book.

I would also like to thank my mentor Jessica Provines, PhD, for her influence and willingness to push me further. I would like to express my appreciation for Samantha Tedder, MS and Layna Adams, MS for their support in making the illustrations a reality. Additionally, I would like to extend my thanks to Jan Gilbert Hurst for her help with the initial review and editing of the manuscript.

I am incredibly grateful to all the wonderful peers, professors, mentors, and inspirations along the way. A big thanks to Lily Lai, PsyD, an amazing peer who is always willing to listen. To all my current and former CAPS team members and trainees, WSU Student Wellness Center leadership and staff, thank you all for inspiring me to be better, dream bigger, and to help more every day.

I must also express my heartfelt thanks to the Newton and Killen families for their kindness and encouragement throughout my journey. I am thankful for the encouragement and support from my Leonard, Malooley, and Maloley relatives. I am grateful for the examples set by my grandparents Elaine Leonard and Edward and Sadie Malooley.

Furthermore, I am indebted to my siblings Nicholas, Angelena, and Gabriel for their constant support and willingness to challenge me to grow. I want to thank my seven nieces and nephews who are always a source of joy with their smiles, laughs, and jokes.

Most importantly, I am profoundly grateful to my parents, Kim and Jeannie, for their steadfast guidance, support, and unwavering faith in me from the beginning. Their encouragement from the beginning has empowered me to achieve more than I ever thought possible.

.

About the Author

Christopher Leonard is a Licensed Psychologist. Dr. Leonard received his Doctor of Psychology degree from Spalding University in 2014. He has been in leadership positions in higher education since 2017. Dr. Leonard has held the positions of an associate director/clinical director and director in university counseling centers. He has over a decade of experience providing therapy and supervising therapists in training.

He has presented locally, regionally, and nationally on a variety of psychological topics, including workplace wellness. One of Dr. Leonard's greatest passions is his work as one of the co-founders of Wichita State University's Suspenders4Hope program, a comprehensive suicide prevention training program that has been adopted by universities and local and regional industries across the United States. As the original "Dr. Suspenders," he knows firsthand how supportive relationships can instill hope in individuals and communities.

Dr. Leonard was the 2025 recipient of the Wichita State University Wayne Carlisle Distinguished Service Award. In 2025, he received the inaugural Transformational Leader Award from the Wichita State University Division of Student Affairs.

In his free time, Dr. Leonard is an avid runner and enjoys the arts. Most importantly, he is blessed with a wonderful supportive family.

You can find Dr. Leonard on LinkedIn and at:
www.flinthillspublishing.com/authors/christopher-leonard

www.ingramcontent.com/pod-product-compliance
Lightning Source LLC
Chambersburg PA
CBHW050025040726

47599CB00015B/1542